30 Seconds Flat

The ShyGuy's Guide to Getting Girls

GREGORY P. WILLIAMS

WRITERS REPUBLIC L.L.C.
515 Summit Ave. Unit R1
Union City, NJ 07087, USA

Website: *www.writersrepublic.com*
Hotline: *1-877-656-6838*
Email: *info@writersrepublic.com*

Ordering Information:
Quantity sales. Special discounts are available on quantity purchases by corporations, associations, and others. For details, contact the publisher at the address above.

Library of Congress Control Number: 2024932313
ISBN-13:   979-8-89100-253-1   [Paperback Edition]
                    979-8-89100-653-9   [Hardback Edition]
                    979-8-89100-254-8   [Digital Edition]

Rev. date: 03/25/2024

To my wife for her unwavering support. Without her this guide could not have been written.

CONTENTS

About the Author

When first I set out to find what love, sex, and life were all about, I was fourteen years old and growing up rapidly. I survived the Oakland, California, riots of the sixties, as well as the sex, drug, and alcohol culture of the sixties, seventies, and eighties. I lived through Southeast Asia during the Vietnam War and came out with a whole new perspective on life.

When I was seventeen and, in the war, if you wanted to get laid, some female would walk up to you and say something like, "Two dolla saily, two dolla ... me love you long time!" Needless to say, this sailor kept a lot of two-dollar bills in his wallet!

I didn't grow up begging girls for anything. I found that sex was my right, and I set out to make life right for myself. This guide is a compilation of the life experiences of people who have come in and out of my life (from the postman to the pimp around the way, and the various women I've met and interviewed, and I've known madams who ran cathouses), plus my personal experiences. And that's a lot of knowledge.

Introduction

The road from ShyGuy to social butterfly will sometimes be paved with humor, laughter and those times when you'll roll your eyes up and shake your head wondering just how did that happen?! I'm Gregory P. Williams and I'll be your tour guide on this roller coaster ride called dating. I wasn't always confident and poised, oh no! However, with practice I found myself being able to talk to any girl (or anyone for that matter) about anything and in any situation. I used to be a ShyGuy just like you until I learned, as I'll hit on later, just how to entice women and girls to come to me. So, climb aboard my fellow ShyGuys and be sure to buckle your seat belt because here we go! The reasons for picking up and studying this guide are varied and only you can know for sure.

However, they probably range anywhere from mere curiosity to desperation and everything else in between. But just as no two women are alike, it follows that no two ShyGuys are alike insofar as their goals and dreams are concerned. Some of us are looking for wives, others are in search of that elusive girlfriend and some of us just want a one-night stand ... every night! (can you say hoochie mama?) However, when those moments appear and she's standing in front of you, if you're anything like I was, it's like there's a demonic spring beneath your tongue that goes booiiing and forces your tongue up to the roof of your mouth. This magical spring then holds your tongue captive until she gets tired of standing there looking at you looking at her and waiting for you to say something then goes on her merry way. Another one bites the dust. But hey, look on the brighter side; she was probably a serial dater anyway and besides, who did her hair, 'Cut's be us?'

Now everything in this guide is in general because there are always exceptions to any rule although for the most part these things hold true. Let's take a case in point: here we have this girl, attractive and apparently intelligent and we have two guys; one is pretty much underfoot showing her love and affection and in every way shows her that he cares. Women can sense when you're hungry and by that I mean desperate so don't act hungry. Now the other fella is standing over there totally aloof and ignoring her, giving her no sign that he even knows she exists much less cares about her. And wouldn't you know it, quicker than water'll make a duck wet, she trips and falls over everything in her path trying to get to the one who doesn't care about her at all! Go figure. Then there are the girls, and we know who you are, who insist on a challenge. Now as far as I know, a challenge is something competitive like boxing or racing where someone wins and someone loses.

Now go figure why a woman would want that type of thing in her relationships, and then when she loses, the first thing she hollers is that all men are dogs as she earnestly and with rare gusto goes happily in search of another just like him. And don't we see evidence of that all the time? It really isn't any wonder then that we ShyGuys get left out in the cold while the playa and the jock are having the time of their lives but that ends here. We deserve the best that life has to offer and from now on we're going to go out there and get what's ours, but buyer beware; it may sound contradictory but to get her you have to act as if you really don't care all that much if she comes or goes. The problem with that is this: act as if you don't care long enough and eventually you won't. But hey, that's who she wants right? So, what is a ShyGuy to do when he finds that beautiful heartthrob that he wants to take home to meet mom?

When first we spy that lovely creature from across the room and our heart starts to pound faster and faster, and our pulse threatens to explode in our veins. And oh GOD, our throat is tightening up and

Gregory P. Williams

we need a drink badly; we must first take a deep breath in through the nose and out through the mouth, a couple of times grasshoppa. Now it's time to ascertain the situation e.g., is anyone with her. If so, who? Did you notice other guys coming and going in her direction as if they're trying to get noticed? Do not just blindly plod over to her as if she were a grape on the vine just ripe for the plucking. Look around and take notice of who's noticing her and who she is noticing. Take in the interplay of everyone around then calmly and purposefully make your way in her direction. By taking in the situation, we can most times ascertain whether she has that 'I'm pretty and I know it' attitude or whether she may be thinking that there are lots of guys to talk to and choose from.

While walking over to her the room seems to have gotten smaller than it should be, the lights are suddenly way too bright, and you know that when the moment comes to speak it'll be bright enough and quiet enough for everyone to hear and see you. Stop it! You're killin' me over here Lol The room is the same size as it was when you first walked in. The lights haven't changed and not to impugn or otherwise bruise your ego, but very probably no one other than she will even notice that you're speaking to her except maybe those jealous fellas eyeballin' you over there who didn't have the nerve to do what you just did or the other women who wished you'd spoken to them.

The words are already in your head because you've rehearsed them and you're ready to go. You've already prepared for this moment; you're dressed to kill because like ZZ TOP says, every woman likes to see a sharp dressed man! She won't be able to do anything other than look at you and smile at what she sees. You want all her senses alive and alert, you don't want her to crinkle up her nose because she smells you coming three feet away. Even the very best colognes reek when put on too heavily (at least in my opinion). A lady friend of mine uses what she calls the spray, delay, then walk away method. Once showered and lotioned, she will spray her perfume over her head, let it settle on her a bit then walk away. Ok now, we're back and looking at her looking at you and ... STOP! This scenario is where you should be at by the time you finish studying this guide. You should be able to fight down your inner fears and walk straight up to Ms Might be Wonderful and say something that'll excite her imagination, something that maybe she's never heard before!

CHAPTER ONE

My Resume and What to Expect

Now I wouldn't say that I'm an expert on how to beguile women, but I will say that I have more feathers in my cap than a hawk has on his backside! I could cite the sheer numbers, but most people probably wouldn't believe me anyway. But to touch on the subject let's just say that I was trying to beat out Wilt Chamberlain! And for those of you who don't know, Wilt Chamberlain topped out at around twenty thousand if the things I have heard are true!

My experience started when I was in the tenth grade and started hanging around older guys who made it their business to know women and they, for lack of a better phrase showed me the ropes. Since that time, I have been a sailor sailing the seven seas and conquering women from all over the world and I truly believe that I've sampled just about everything this world has to offer. After that I lived in the San Francisco / Oakland Bay Area where the girls in the city sho look pretty. I mean I almost hurt myself there were so many girls coming and going in and out of my place like it had a revolving door! These days I'm a little older and work as a Freight Train Conductor taking trains from here to there then back again. This gives me the opportunity to talk to women from all over the country and prove to myself that what I've learned in this life about women still holds true! As I said earlier, the absolute numbers of the women I've had gives this guide more information and authority than other books on the subject (at least in my opinion). I've written this guide in a manner that makes it easy to read and understand. Now maybe you have bought and /or read books that you thought would help clear the muddy waters but really did little more than dirty the waters even more. Well, this time you've gotten yourself a manual, a 'how-to' roadmap that will lead you step by interesting step through the tangled world of dating.

The information I've assembled here comes from people from all types of occupations and styles of life, including my own personal experiences. People I've known from the local postal worker to the pimp around the way; from girls I've run across and interviewed, to madams in cat houses who were kind and generous enough to give me a thought or two on the matter. The information gathered here is a compilation of the thoughts and experiences of many individuals from different lifestyles. If your love life is anything like mine was then you're in need of a little romance, you deserve it!

Romance is more than just sex; it's a feeling that makes you feel alive and vibrant. Romance makes you think there isn't anything in this world that you can't do. It's wonderful but hard to find experience unless you know the when, where, and how to achieve it. Understanding this manual will give you more confidence than you ever thought possible. Confidence in not just dating but in all other areas of your life as well. You'll no longer be as nervous as a long-tailed cat in a room full of rocking chairs. Along with confidence comes character (that is, if you have a conscience). Character is that trait that draws people to you. I have seen men who were once homeless due to circumstances, but because of their character and confidence were able to greatly improve their standing in life and are now as we say out on the rails, 'livin' the dream'. By the time you're done you'll no longer be a zero but some beautiful woman's hero!

There have been more books than I can remember seeing on the subjects of dating and confidence and the like. I've gone out and bought and read several of them myself. The things that they talked about intrigued me at first but for some reason I could never see a clear-cut path to my goals. This manual on the other hand, not only addresses the needs of we ShyGuys but also those wants that we so desperately wish for. Imagine walking up to someone you find attractive and alluring then just start talking to her, watching her eyes light up with amusement and happiness because here is someone who knows how to speak to a woman, addressing her desires without her knowing that's what you're doing. Can you say SUAVE?

Endless are the possibilities that you can achieve once you've studied this guide. You've noticed by now that I say, 'study & guide' and not 'read & book' The key to success is understanding what makes them tick and that's what you'll learn here so don't just read this -study it! And you will find that one of the easiest ways to get the girl you want is to be around her while being charming with the other females and totally ignoring her. She will wonder why you're not all over her pretty little self like the other guys are. Uh oh, you've just become a 'challenge' look out!

However, before all this is possible, we must take a closer look at what makes us ShyGuys to begin with and to overcome those shortcomings and fears. We ShyGuys were not born that way, and by that, I mean we didn't come out of our mothers afraid to speak, on the contrary, we made all sorts of sounds and noises. We learned this shy behavior somewhere along the highways and by-ways of life. As for myself I used to try to talk to the opposite sex, but they would either not talk to me, talk about me or just laugh at me. After enough times of that happening, I began to become quieter and quieter until it got to the point that when so-called 'friends' would ask me for my last dollar I was too shy to say "no", shame can do a lot of damage to a person's ego. These days not only can I say no to someone, but I can say hell no!

Then there is the fear of rejection which led me to speak even less to a girl. I mentioned the older fellas who helped me see the light and here's what I learned in a nutshell; it's an ancient oriental proverb. "Chase a butterfly and it flies from you but turn your attention to other things and it gently lands on your shoulder!" After I learned to stop chasing the butterfly as it were, I would quite often find that it (love and romance) landed on my shoulder on the regular! The qualities we would like to have are confidence and charm with a little bit of suave thrown in for good measure. These qualities are not very difficult to attain given the untapped resources now at your fingertips.

I used to be totally without charm or confidence and talk about being suave ... NOT! So, I went in search of and eventually found the secret to becoming those things and do you know what? You too can have these characteristics if you only set your mind to it with all the determination at your command. When you see most other guys with gorgeous women it usually isn't because they're particularly charming or anything, it's because they have something the woman wants and/or needs like a nice home, a big car, lots of money, and let's not forget, females tend to be preternaturally drawn to 'pretty' boys', no matter how functionally illiterate they may be etc. With the techniques you will learn here you'll be able to get the girl because of you and not external conditions.

By now you are probably asking yourself 'self', just how long will all this take? I mean it took me a lifetime to get here, so how long will it take to get there? My answer to that is it depends on how badly you want it! If you are willing to put in some work, get out there and work on some of the exercises laid out in this manual, you'll have it down pat in no time at all. It's kinda like cooking a cake, put in all the right ingredients and give the bowl a good twirl with the spoon then put it in the oven and let it bake. Right now, you are at the part where you're reading the instructions on the side of the box. Next, you will be at the place where you're mixing all the ingredients together, then finally you'll put it in the oven and what comes out may surprise you. You'll be charming and witty, a good conversationalist and listener. Girls will enjoy being around you!

How many times did we wish that our love lives would improve or wish that it would just BE anything other than what it is now? My

 Gregory P. Williams

love life improved when I began to stop wishing for it and decided to do something about it although for me that 'something' came about almost by accident. Love doesn't usually just come to you although that does happen on occasion. Look at how it came to me; it came through at least some kind of effort on my part. Until now we have used all of the wrong methods to create that awe-inspiring love life that we've always dreamed of. Now we can systematically get that marriage, girlfriend, and fun we've always wanted.

It takes just a little bit of knowing how to achieve this but in the end, life will improve greatly, sometimes in ways you've never thought of and isn't this what we all want? For life to give us what we deserve? I've been married more than once and divorced; divorced because I forgot to use the information I've given you in this guide. This guide helped me to get the girl, but I forgot to remember the part about keeping her!

People will begin to notice a slow but sure change in your personality. Where once you were pretty much quiet now, you're participating in all the conversations and heaven forbid you're even handing out your own opinion! You will notice that people seem to be more attracted to you ... both male and female. Why is that you may ask yourself? It is because you're beginning to create a magnetic personality! The thing is, the more you practice the ideas I've laid out for you the more magnetic your personality will become! How about the worry you used to have about that prom date? No more, that issue is resolved.

And the girl who wouldn't speak to you? Now you have found you don't have time for her. My personality changed to the point that guys started to become envious of me! Why? Because I had learned to do what they only dreamed of being able to do. I remember once when a 'friend' of mine and I were out and about when we both looked up and saw this attractive young woman sitting across the way in the lounge we had found ourselves at. I said, "hey, let's go over there and introduce ourselves" he replied, "Gregory, you just can't walk up to a woman and do that" hmm ... I got up and walked over to her, introduced myself and bought us both a drink then left with her about an hour later! My 'friend' just looked at me with wonder as his jaw dropped to the floor ... Lol. After that he didn't want to be friends with me anymore. Oh well, tough titty said the cat to the kitty. Wouldn't you like to be able to do that too? You can!

What are your odds of success you ask? The odds are all in your favor because you'll be doing and saying things that these strange acting women won't have a clue about. My personal odds went from about zero to right around eighty percent. Now I don't get everyone I go after, but I do get my share of them and that's not including those who come after me! All this may seem impossible to you my fellow ShyGuys, but I assure you it's not. It's all within your reach and if I can do it (I've never been a pretty man, I'm what women have called 'ruggedly handsome', whatever that means) then you can too! Once you have become comfortable in your own skin and realize that these women aren't all that you will see an increase in your numbers. A side note here; pretty girls are about the easiest to get, especially if they are pretty and shy. I'll get to that a little later. Just be sure you really want all the female attention you'll be getting!

Each chapter is built upon the previous one sorta like when you're learning to play chess. You first learn what the pieces are then you learn how to move them; the when, where, and how to make them. I did this in order for you, my fellow ShyGuys, to get one building stone then another until you have a solid foundation to stand on. Once you lay the foundation, should the building fall for some out of the way reason, it can be re-built using the same foundation. Things won't always go according to plan but once again just like chess should you make a wrong move you can always recover and come out ahead of the game! Life has taught me that having a clear-cut goal is like riding a bike; if you know where you're going it doesn't matter if you have a flat or fall because you do know where you're going and you can always fix that flat, get back up and keep on riding or just start walking. On the other hand, having no clear-cut goal is like trying to sit on the bike with both feet on the pedals and not moving ... you can see how you could easily become neurotic!

Since we're on the subject and taking the analogy of chess further, there is the opening game where you make your first move, preparing for what's to follow. Then there's the middle game where you're making all those smooth moves, maneuvering your way closer to her. Then we have the end game where that sweet little thing falls desperately into your arms. I know it sounds simple and it really is, although there is some strategy involved. You must maneuver her here then there, getting into the right position to capture her heart! You never get a second chance to make a first impression so in the opening you're at your absolute best, dressed to the nines and smelling sweeter than a New York City hooker, plus you're more charming and suave than Don Juan. In the middle game you give her the reason to move past that first impression and now she's decided to stick around for act three. The end game is where that curious and astonished cutie finally lets down her guard and invites you to come into her world. Checkmate. Yanno, getting the girl isn't all that difficult once you've learned certain rules and techniques.

They're about as predictable as rain is on a real cloudy and overcast day. Keeping the girl is yet another subject, but one that we'll talk about later. It's like I said, 'they' are so predictable. You can achieve whatever your goal is simply by first stating it on paper. Once you have put your goal on paper and in exact detail, you've gone from having a thought to having a concrete version of that thought right there in your hand! Along with that detailed goal you will have written a 'business plan' stating precisely what it is you want and how you are going to go about getting it; your thoughts have now become 'real'. Once you've begun to execute your plan, you'll be happily surprised to find that she's almost working the plan for you. Women just need a little subliminal guidance to get with the program and as Forest Gump would say 'and that's all I have to say about that!' At least for the moment.

There is a spark of something in you already or wouldn't be ready to study this manual. That spark of something is quite probably a little thing called hope. All you need now is the confidence that this guide will give you to reach higher than you ever thought possible. At this moment it doesn't matter at what point you're at in life, but what does matter is that you've taken this important first step on the road to self-fulfillment. The method found here is tried and true, tested and proven by me over a lifetime so be confident in the outcome and in yourself because if you give the effort the payoff will be a new and brighter future. I've been sadder than a man should ever have to be and happier than I could ever imagine, but through it all these ideas that I've written down for you, my fellow ShyGuys, have always held true. So, tip a glass of your favorite beverage and give yourself a toast to the future. Ready? Let's do this!

Gregory P. Williams

CHAPTER TWO

What We Want from Them

To me, honesty comprises many facets from truth naturally, to sharing and caring, loving, giving etc. I personally need Ms Right to be honest in all these areas so that I won't have the need to go and find Ms Right Now ... right now! A lot of women you will find out here are deceptive to the point of I wouldn't trust them as far as I can see, and I can't see all that well without my glasses! Oh, and haven't we ShyGuys run across those fraudulent females who swear they don't like us but every time you turn around, she's peeping at you out of the corner of her eye. Then there are the ones who apparently without thought, consideration or regard for we ShyGuys, perpetrate dishonesty in all their romances which is why you'll occasionally run into the serial dater. Therefore, honesty should be at the top of your list. If she will be dishonest about trivial matters, how honest do you think she will be about something truly important?

Regarding kindness, let me just say that kindness is truly in the eye of the beholder. Some ShyGuys think a kind woman is one who we can put up in a shrine and admire with awe but beware, if you put a gold crown on her head, you'll likely be the first one she beheads but hey, maybe you like it rough like that. There are some of us who think kindness is being stepped on with six-inch spiked heels... who am I to playa hate? Like I always say, whatever floats ya boat! Then there are the rest of us who believe kindness is someone considerate and forgiving to a fault, warm and loving. I like a woman who wakes me up with a whisper of my name and a gentle rub on my arm. For me, kindness is gentleness mixed with some understanding. Whatever it is to you just make sure that she is what you need her to be because if you don't go after what you want, you'll end up settling for what you can get. Although getting the girl is certainly a win, wanting to keep her around is truly uplifting to your soul. I've had girls who were kind until they thought they had me on a leash then the real girl came out. Their eyes would start to spin and glow satanically, and their heads would spin around and doggone if they didn't try to sink those sharp fangs into my neck! Get thee from me o' foul thing I would shout as I grabbed a wooden stake!

Just how sexy you want Ms Lady to be depends entirely on you since sexy is a relative term. She can be as sexy as a super model or as demure as a preacher's wife, whatever it is that brings out that desire in you. There is nothing worse, at least in my opinion, than getting the girl then finding out too late that she's a closet prude (then again, prude might be right up your alley!). That excitement you want must come from someone who has that trait inherent to her personality, so make sure from the start that Ms Girlie has those qualities innate to her being. Wouldn't you like to open the door and immediately feel that desire to hold her? You can if you follow a few simple steps to living a new and better life. Sexy can be the way she walks or that little giggle in her voice when she talks or maybe it's the way her eyes sparkle when she looks into yours.

A reasonable girl is kinda hard to find so if you do find her keep her. Too often, girls look at things in the most unreasonable ways that we ShyGuys can imagine. I like a clever and quick-witted woman myself, one that can keep up with me and be able to hold an interesting and meaningful conversation. At this point let me just say that if you run across a girl who says 'conversate', run man ... run fast and run far! Cause dayuum, girl got issues. Another trait is understanding. Understanding what you are and who she is. See, we men were born to hunt and kill, protect, and provide while they were born to nurture and love. If she is intelligent enough to understand that then you've got yourself a winner cause that hound 'sho can hunt. Relationships should be the kind where both parties protect the feelings of the other from outsiders.

I had a girl who didn't do that, and it ended up being a bad deal. Why? Because I felt that she should've stood up and told her family and friends this is my man chill out. On the other side of the coin, I was doing exactly what I was supposed to have been doing, telling my family that this is my girl so don't disrespect her. Some people find it hard to say no to someone and I completely understand because there was a time when I couldn't say no either. But with practice you'll be able to say not only no but hell no. Plus the added attraction of being able to teach her how to do the same thing. For we ShyGuys, romance is the ending or the beginning if you like, of a long and inspiring journey.

Romance and sex are not always the same thing so do not get them confused. See, you can hook up with a hooker from Houston, do your thing and leave ... no romance. On the other hand, if you have romance you have it all. Romance will make you feel as if you're taller and bigger than you really are. Romance is food to the soul just as corn flakes are food to the body. I love that soulful feeling that comes from deep down inside that gives me a whole new different outlook and attitude about life and living. I think about those amorous feelings that well up from doing nothing more than holding hands.

Some of us need affection, not all of us but most of us. It's that warm and giddy feeling that comes from our yet to be girlfriend. You can see the caring and sharing light up in her eyes by the way she touches and caresses your hand. We ShyGuys appreciate tenderness from a woman more so than most men. Most men just take it for granted whereas we hold that feeling deep in our hearts. Just as we expect and want warmth and caring from her, we must always be ready to give those things in return, but we must know how to show those feelings in a unique way. Because if you start being all warm and fuzzy, she will think you weak and will happily run all over you the way a track star runs over hurdles. We must maintain that

I really don't care all that much if you come or go attitude while at the same time kissing her gently on the back of her neck. Kinda like a politician pinching a baby's cheek with one hand while stealing his lollipop with the other!

A girl who loves her mother is a wonderful thing yes indeed, because if she doesn't love mom how is she ever supposed to be able to love you? It shows that she has priorities in her life and is not like someone who doesn't know where she is going. We ShyGuys tend to love our moms and be Mama's boys so to speak and can appreciate a girl who does the same thing. There's something gentle in her nature which goes back to sharing and caring. Loving. Learning from mom has taught her to be and for lack of better terms obedient and submissive to your needs and there is nothing wrong with that see, mom has taught her a woman's role in the grand scheme of things so yes, loving mom is a trait I'd definitely go for.

For those of us who want kids, having a girl who shares the same views is important. There is nothing worse than wanting something from your spouse and she isn't having it. There's nothing like a pack of crumb snatchers running around the house making it feel more like a home. Knowing your bloodline will continue is an important thing too. Did you know that after an earthquake or some other disaster there's an increase in childbirth in the affected area approximately nine months later? just thought I'd take a moment for some statistics. Okay, I'm back and where were we? Oh yes, kids ... Those darling little rug rats tugging on your pant pockets looking for a few pennies ... Did I say pennies? I forgot for a moment that this isn't my childhood because these days they want dollars!

Let's move on to the subject of just how attractive a woman has to be. We all want a pretty girl, but beauty is truly in the eyes of the beholder and let's face it, the world isn't filled with just pretty girls, ya got the other ones too. For me, she just has to be attractive enough that I can walk down the street with her and still be able to hold my head up and smile at passersby! Have you ever seen a woman so unattractive that she was actually cute? Well, I once dated this girl

    Gregory P. Williams

who was just that and I mean coyote ugly and oh, on the off chance you don't know what coyote ugly is here you go; a coyote when caught in a trap will chew his own leg off to get free. When you wake up with a really bad hangover from the night before and you have got this bugga-bear lying next to you in your arms, it makes you want to chew your own arm so you can leave without waking her up!

Anyways, she once said to me, "you must think I'm ugly cause you only come to see me at night" and I replied "no honey, it's just that I like the way the stars shine in your eyes" well hey, ya gotta be able to blow smoke at them at a moment's notice. Or have you ever seen a not bad looking man with that Wolverine on his arm and you wonder just how did that happen? He loves her but somebody cut that chicken off at the neck! You're probably looking for someone who is tantalizing and alluring, a girl with that magic walk that you just can't get enough of watching. But be careful here because behind that lovely face could lurk a rafter hanging from vampira just waiting to suck your wallet dry! There is a little side note I'd like to put here, like my old man used to say, "follow an ugly child home and something ugly'll open the door".

Next on the list is a cheerful girl, someone who smiles easily and is always happy at least most of the time. Who wants a sour Puss? Someone who when she walks inside, the whole room lights up as if the sun had somehow fallen down and crept in. A girl who is optimistic and glad most of the time. Wouldn't you like to open the front door and there she is just standing there and smiling at you because she's glad and happy to see your smiling face. I like a girl who can make me sparkle from the other side of the phone. She sounds almost impossible, doesn't she? But she's not! She's someplace that you've already been or will shortly be showing up at. So, when she does show up, you'll be at your absolute best game.

A generous woman once again, is about the best because she's generous with everything so be careful not to use and abuse her by accident or on purpose. We ShyGuys want a girl who is giving in every way, her love, affection, time etc. We desire someone who shares her innermost thoughts without hesitation so that you always know what's on her mind and never have to guess. Someone who is willing to give of herself while at the same time willing to accept you as you are with all your shortcomings and defaults. You'll have to weed through a lot of women to find this treasure unless you're lucky enough to find her from the gate. She'll make loving her as easy as making a peach cobbler! That is if you can cook!

Most people are useful to a certain degree, then you have those who are completely useless. Take for an example the woman who is intelligent, attractive and keeps herself up but that's as far as it goes. She can't cook, she can't clean the house and the only thing she knows about cars is to put gas in them and let's hope she doesn't burn up the engine!

She's sometimes referred to as a trophy wife, outwardly she's everything a fella could ask for but dayuum, that hound sho caint hunt. So, make sure she has skills other than just looking good because eventually she'll just be an anchor pulling you down into the depths. A good cook is hard to find these days. They tell me that down south a skinny woman can't get a man although the big girls are in high demand, the reason? Men figure the girl is skinny because she can't cook and the big girl... well, there's something comforting about a good hot meal prepared by a big pretty woman. Also, if she is a good cook, odds are she's into pleasing her man by keeping him healthy and happy. Imagine going over to her house and opening the door to be greeted with the aromas of cake and ham hocks with collard greens and some hot water cornbread! And for those of you who do not know, that's some mighty fine dining! So, my fellow ShyGuys, find yourselves a good cook cause good kissin' don't last, but good cookin' do!

There's nothing worse, at least to me, than a woman with her hand out. I mean come on, you have to bring to the table at least what I'm bringing. She's gotta have a job or be self-employed, either way she has to be trying to be successful in life. The only thing a woman like that is missing is a good man ... Someone like we ShyGuys. Money

     Gregory P. Williams

in and of itself doesn't amount to a thing, it's the freedom that cold hard cash can afford you. Having a girl with a job means you can buy each other things, go traveling together or just hang out at the local jazz lounge. If she doesn't have a source of income, she'll look toward you to pay her way which isn't a bad thing unless you're doing it all the time. Here's a little math: you have money+ she doesn't = you coming up short!

I put self-reliance high on the list because I've learned that a woman who isn't self-reliant has to rely on you. That's not a terrible thing if you truly have love and affection for the girl. I've had to step away from more than a few girls who were holding their hands out. Kinda sad really, I liked a couple of them, but I couldn't live my lifestyle and support theirs at the same time. Somebody had to go. C'ya!

CHAPTER THREE

Falling in Love vs. Falling in Lust

We all define fulfillment in differing ways, for some of us it's lying on the beach on a warm spring day and for others it's a sense of joy and happiness that comes from buying that first home. We ShyGuys like the beach as much as anyone else and we like owning homes and things like that but for the lack of a better phrase we lust after love which by the way is our biggest thrill and biggest mistake. Falling in love versus falling in lust, now there's a double-edged sword for you. On the one hand there is the love of your life and on the other hand there is Ms Right Now with her sexy little self. Either way we are in search of some kind of fulfillment in our lives.

There's this big hole we ShyGuys are trying desperately to fill. As we talked about earlier, love is that feeling that makes you think you can rule the world while on the other hand, lust is that feeling that makes you feel as if you're ready to be every woman's King! Sometimes lust is a healthy thing because you don't need to be in love in order to feel good about someone, conversely, you don't necessarily need to be lusting to be in love. Each of us has a different view of what constitutes fulfillment. For me, it's a happy balance between love and lust because I love lusting after my sweetie.

     Gregory P. Williams

Some people love to like while others like to love, and the biggest difference is ... Absolutely none that I can see. Love, as we talked about earlier, is that feeling that makes you feel as if you are at the top of the world while lust on the other hand is more of a trusting with your feelings kinda thing. I once fell in love with a woman I couldn't stand but later I fell in like with a woman I could've married. I think that love is more of a mind thing with like being more of a heart affliction, at least it has been like that in my life. If you find someone that gives you that love feeling, then go for it and if you find someone that gives you that I've found my searched for friend feeling then go for that. It's that craving we ShyGuys have for romantic pleasures although others look for the same thing, it seems that we search for it even harder.

Some people find that falling in love is something you do over a period of time; they say you have to be friends first then you find love then you find marriage although I've found that marriage can often ruin a good friendship. Falling in love means acceptance of the other person's good traits as well as bad habits. I know I said a little while ago that love and like are about the same thing but let me just back up a minute and say that love sometimes means you don't really have a tolerance for the other person's faults while with friends, we seem to be more tolerant.

Lust is the first sign of liking someone, you start to fall in lust by first looking across the way at that gorgeous little thing sitting over there with her bare legs crossed talking to that other gorgeous little thing. You imagine that you can almost see that camel's toe beneath that slinky form fitting dress she's wearing. When first we lust, our imaginations begin to run amok with intense desires of touching, caressing, and running our fingers through her luscious weave! Then feeling her warm soft body lying against ours. I need a cigarette cause that was good to me! Okay, I'm back. Now where were we? Oh yeah, after we have begun lusting after Ms lovely we then formulate our plan for letting her, let us into her world.

The side effects of love versus lust are thinking you're in love and the other person is not, then you end up walking down a one-way Street. If on the other hand, you're in lust and she is not, then you end up on a different one-way Street. These adverse effects are dependent on who is and who is not in love and or lust. These undesirable side effects can be minimized by not feeling any emotion in either direction. Remember, she wants what she thinks she can't have so she's going to do the exact opposite of what you're saying so if you want love then act like you don't. And if you want lust then behave as if lusting after her is the last thing on this earth you want to do. She'll shake off her panties faster than hot grease will fry bacon.

The right reasons for wanting love or lust are pretty much obvious considering you're sitting here in your PJs reading this manual. Less obvious is that deep-seated need for companionship and love/lust but mostly the right reasons are right there in your heart and mind. But be careful, as we talked about earlier, about what it is you truly want.

The wrong reasons for love or lust are those having to do with a letdown. We must not seek love or lust simply because Ms Baby ripped our heart from our chest and we're feeling that deep, dank, and empty void. Always remember, girls are like city buses; one comes by every twenty minutes so don't get down in the dumps. She may have been someone you might've found yourself not wanting or needing anyway.

Which is best, love or lust? I don't know about you, but I personally just love to lust after that sexy little cutie, but that's me. Believe it or not, there are some of us who think love is the answer to everything. See, you can be in love and still be unhappy while on the other hand you can be in lust with someone who is in love with you and then you walk through fire together. There's that excitement that leaves you smiling and wanting to come back for more, and for me that's contentment.

The human need for love is a strange and baffling thing indeed. We humans can have everything in the world at our fingertips but still feel empty without love. What is it about that little four-letter word? Because I can think of another four-letter word that can easily replace love. But then again that's just me. Okay seriously now, I also have the need for love, that forlorn and sometimes happy feeling that fills up your heart.

The need for lust is just as strong as the need for love. And I mean fabulously freaky with absolutely no boundaries. I suppose you can tell by now that this once ShyGuy prefers lust over love. If I can have both at the same time then all is well and good, but if given the choice I go for the nasty girl every time. Old pimps say that you can't turn a hoe into a housewife, but I believe that a reformed and recovering hoe makes for the best wife because she's been there and done that. She's been with different men and knows the various types so when she chooses you, you can be sure that she has picked through the pack until she found you!

Some of us fall in love while others simply choose to be in love, the same holds true for lust. To fall or not to fall, that is the question, isn't it? With the one we're completely helpless and pretty much swinging in the wind, going wherever and whichever way the breeze blows us. By choosing to be in love or lust, we can maintain some semblance of control over our destiny. So, in one instance we're aware and in the other we're helpless and blind like those mice we were told about as children. So yes, there's a huge difference between the two so choose carefully.

A funny thing happened the other day, a fellow ShyGuy asked me was there a difference in the divorce rate between those in love and those of us in lust. I said to myself I said 'self', isn't that an interesting question. And so, I went in search of an answer and what I found was a whole lot different from what I thought it would be. It appears, at least from what I found, that a relationship based on straight up lust lasted longer than those in love. It seems that when you're getting your swerve on regularly it tends to make you happier than when your heart's merely content. Now don't get me wrong ShyGuys I'm not advocating that you go out there and sex everyone you can, I'm just saying ...

Now onto the subject of which makes us the happiest. So, what is it that makes you happy in a relationship? Is it good sex every day or is it love and commitment? I've had people say to me that you can have both at the same time and that's very much true ... In some instances. For some strange reason men will sex the one they like then take home to mom the one they merely love! Now I don't know about you, but I'd rather have the one I like as opposed to the one I love because love is blind as a bat. You can be totally in love with a woman you can't stand and, conversely, you can be in lust with someone you truly like, so you be the judge.

Maybe it's just me but I think that lust is a whole lot more fun than love. It seems like every time I was in love, we'd do that boot knockin' dance in the bedroom which by the way is the last place I want to be. Conversely, when I was in lust, we would do that dance everywhere but in the bedroom! I sometimes wondered why I couldn't find love and lust in the same package. Just like most other guys I'd go for the bad girl then take the good girl home to meet mom. Until one day a thirty-second conversation got me that special one see, I was out and about when I heard car horns blaring and tires squealing, I looked up and saw Ms Lovely crossing the street. Strangely enough she was walking in my direction, so I started walking toward her ... After my thirty-second spiel I had her name and number and we both fell deeply in lust and didn't we have a really good time. I will get to the importance of that initial thirty seconds a little later.

 Gregory P. Williams

Chapter Four

Rebounded Love

Rebounding from love is like a basketball bouncing off the rim; there's no telling where it's going to end up. There's this emptiness that you feel deep down inside like your soul has a toothache. You just need to fill it with something ... Anything at all and that's where the problems start. Rebound syndrome has caused more pain than the dentist! One the worst things you can do fellas is to get with someone simply because you have no one. When you do that, you end up with the wrong person almost every time.

You only think that is love but you're only filling the void and filling it with whatever you can. I've gotten with someone because of rebound syndrome and what happened was that when Ms I've Been Waiting for You showed up, I couldn't get with her because I was already with someone else and this ShyGuy still feels the pain. Why didn't I leave her you may ask, and my answer is this; I was feeling what I thought was love but in reality it was me rebounding from a previous relationship and just like that basketball I ended up somewhere else.

People fall in love sometimes for the wrong reasons. Sadness is the main culprit with loneliness being a close second. Sometimes we fall in like and mistake it for love. When you're in emotional pain it's very easy to meet up with someone and open your heart up like you're opening up a can of tuna. We ShyGuys must keep a close vigilance on why we're feeling what we're feeling so as not to get caught up in a trap that may be hard to free ourselves from. Sadness is something we can deal with simply by realizing what it is we are sad about. The same thing holds true for loneliness. There have been times when I thought I couldn't get any sadder and then there were times when I felt that the loneliness was going to eat me from the inside. What l found is that external and wrong reasons for falling in love can be discovered and dealt with.

Another sign of the vicious and cruel circle of rebound syndrome is you giving way too much of yourself whereas Ms Taking You for Granted isn't giving much at all. There's an old saying that goes like this 'fair exchange is no robbery' meaning that when both are giving equally then no harm no foul. But when one is giving more than the other then a crime is being committed against your heart. You can tell if you're going through rebound syndrome by taking note of how you feel. Do you feel as if you're giving too much? Is she not giving back? Are you feeling used? Are you being taken for granted? If you answered yes to any of these questions, then you're probably in a rebounded relationship.

The flip side of the coin is that if she is rebounding and let me tell you ... dayuum, she is all over you like flies on doo doo. I mean she will have you feeling smothered but in this case the smothering feels so good. But the bad part of that is that she is in it for all the wrong reasons. Something is very wrong when Ms Girley says she can't breathe because you're holding on too tight. If we care too much it appears to her that we're holding on too tight, and the funny thing is that when we stop holding on at all she's all over you, which is wrong. She is as happy as can be.

Oftentimes the fear of losing her will cause us to put the big squeeze on the girl. Remember what we talked about earlier? Well, there you are underfoot showing her love and affection and what does she do? She runs away! Women are sometimes Street rat crazy. There's this ancient Native American saying that goes "if you cup

		Gregory P. Williams

your hand in a stream you can hold water, but if you squeeze your fist, you'll lose it all". So be careful not to hold on too tightly.

Then there's the fear of being alone, having no one to talk to or express your feelings to. Especially being in a relationship where you're giving all and she's giving nothing in return like at the casino when you give them all your money and they give you very little back.

Once, a while back after my first wife and I had been divorced for several years, she called me and told me the funniest thing. Well at least it was funny to me. It seems that she had a boyfriend that she had just broken up with for several reasons. He was clingy for one thing (rebound syndrome). One day she heard him outside calling loudly "but I lubded you" and I said "lubded honey?" She said she didn't know he couldn't talk, she thought he was just quiet.

See, she was not rebounding from anything or anyone while he was. He 'lubded' her but she didn't lubded' him back the way that he wanted. He was showing her love and affection, and she was inadvertently walking all over him which, by the way, is the reason I left her in the first place. I was too nice, and she mistook that for weakness so I said "c'ya when I c'ya baby" and got my hat and coat then bounced my way out of her life or should I say I bounced her out of mine.

When you're rebounding, you're trying as hard as you can to be in love like you were before, but that is impossible because your previous relationship is gone, over and dead. You will probably never get it back ... Probably. And now the girl is treating you badly because you're hungry and acting like it. She is under the impression that she can use you like a comfortable and worn old carpet; just walk all over you and that makes you unhappy right? As unhappy as you are you are putting up with what makes the grass grow tall and green. That unhappiness at some point in time turned to anger and Ms Need Some Get Right doesn't understand what it is you're angry about as she continues to use and abuse you like you're a different variety of crack! Here you feel like you're caught in a trap with all the walls, barbed wire and bars. You just don't see a way out. When you get to this point it's time to act like a San Francisco hooker and blow.

But do we leave? Nooo! And doggone it, what has she done now? She's out there clubbing and having herself a really good time. Here's something I've never quite figured out: why does she do these things that you only do to someone you didn't care anything about, and then doesn't leave you? Is she getting some demented thrill out of hurting us? Ms Need Some Medication is strange indeed. And now this fella comes into the picture and she's saying, "he's only just a friend, you just don't understand!" But you grudgingly accept that too! How much dealing with rebound syndrome is enough? When I was going through it, I stopped at the friend part. I said, "you and your friend can kiss my misunderstanding ass". And then there is the lying you're putting up with. The girl lies about everything; if she says it's sunny outside on a summer's day you better go look before you believe her. The warning signs are all there but choose to ignore them at your own peril. Sometimes the signs are subtle but oftentimes it can be as blatant as a flaming queen on main street in Boise Idaho. Rebounded love will have you watching the clock go tick tock tick tock waiting on Ms Running the Streets to bring her cute self home.

Then there are those unexplained little things like that faint hint of a man's Cologne on her or those lunch breaks where she can't be found, and you know the girl likes to have sex, but you don't seem to be getting any lately because she has a headache. That's right fellas, like Johnnie Taylor said "stop doggin me around" and it seems like there is nothing you can do about it and the girl just won't straighten up. So, what's a ShyGuy to do? I'll tell you what to do, shake those feelings like a dog shaking fleas and shake her loose too! When both of you are rebounding from love then ooh wee! You're both out there out of pure desperation and the lovin is sweet, hard, and long lasting. The last time I was in this situation me and Ms Ooh Wee had the time of our lives, dancing and romancing under the moonlit stars. Every time we touched it would be an electric spark jumping from one body to the other. As a side note here fellas, I think people used the term 'soul mate' way too easily because when she and I first met we were finishing each other's sentences and thoughts within a few minutes and instinctively knew what each other liked ... We even kissed alike, now that's a soul mate. She was the female version of me and I the male version of her. She was gorgeous with a female body builders' figure and at that time I was lifting weights too. Sad thing as it turned out was that we were both there out of pure desperation for someone to love. Desperation isn't a good motive, at least in my humble opinion, to be with someone. So be careful.

CHAPTER FIVE

Who Do We Really Want-The Street Rat Crazy Girls (them) A Different Species

Now on to the subject of just who it is that you want because these Street rat crazy girls are an entirely unusual species. There is a plethora, a buffet if you will of girls and their attendant personalities out there ShyGuys. And by that, I mean anything and everything you ever thought or dreamed of having in a woman. She is out there just waiting for you to walk up! Just be careful what and who it is that you ask for because you just might get it. We all have differing measurements we use to gauge a girl and her potential for being able to deliver what we want and need. Should we go after her for her size? Small and petite, big and buxom, thin and shapely ... Curvy ... Whatever you want. Then we must contend with their personalities not to mention their fun meter rating which we'll get to now, and oh my!

The Good Girl

First at bat is the good girl. What is it, we may ask ourselves, that makes a good girl a good girl? Is it her engaging smile and grace? The sincerity with which she speaks to us. Or maybe it's the quiet and gentle nature of her soul and being. Well, that's a whole lot of happy crappy fellas. She's a good girl because she never learned how to be bad! And bad is in her blood, but it's hard to bring it out of her so that makes her a lot of work. Isn't it strange how we'll play with the bad girl because she does what we want but take the so-called good girl home to meet mom. The good girl has a rating of about three on the fun meter scale of one to ten with one being so un-fun that you just can't take it and ten being so much fun that you just can't take it! What can I say, she's a good girl.

The Shy Girl

Now on to the shy girl my brethren in shyness, and what makes her so shy. She's probably a hoe in recovery with lots of bones in her closet and she knows that if she opens her mouth, one just might fall out! Then there are the ones who don't know what to say to a man. They want attention but behave in a manner that says, 'I'm unapproachable'. Most of the time she's just as sweet as grandma's homemade butter and will do almost anything for you insofar as taking care of a man is concerned, that is when she has one. One of my daughters was sitting in her college classroom when one of her classmates, who had never said or did anything to let her know that he was interested - well, one day he walked in and at once started apologizing for the white rose he had for her! Then the poor guy was too scared to say anything else to her and my daughter is one of the sweetest people I know. Too bad. The shy girl gets a whooping four on the fun meter.

The Hood Rat: What Kind of Cheese for Bait, That Is the Question

This lady does not dress particularly sexy or anything but she's what you'd call an 'around the way girl'. Yeah fellas, she's the girl next door or down the way. Baby doesn't have a lot of money but she's fun to be around because she is straight up down to earth. She's highly fascinated with that mighty fine automobile you're driving around town in (Toyota). The girl wouldn't know an expensive luxury car if it jumped up and ran her over. She is content with just living life, but sometimes she can be a drama queen. For fun and games, I give the hood rat a five on the fun meter.

The Gold Digger

Now on to the gold digger and how to spot one. You can tell a gold digger right away because she is blinging brighter than a rap star's platinum and diamond front teeth! Ms Lady is in it to win it 'fo sho'. We men are faced with the dilemma of the gold digger on a regular basis; especially we who are employed, have our own cars and worse, our own place. Now add being famous to this and the digging turns right up! So here are a few tips for spotting those gold mining women who have just one thing on their minds - your pocket and what's in it.

1. She's usually very petty with a lot of attractive female friends. And like I said, she's blinging ... this is how she will first catch your eye. See, something shiny not only catches fish but will catch a guy too!

2. The girl isn't anywhere near shy, so you'll know that she is interested in you. She will tell you everything you want to hear-no one is funnier, sexier, or smarter than you if you let her tell it. If all that glitter and those sweet candy lies take you in and you end up going out with her then watch for these signs, they will show up fairly soon.

   - She starts dropping hints. "Something's wrong with my car, I hope I don't have to take it to the shop cause I just paid my mother's doctor bill" or she'll talk about not having enough money for this and that i.e. rent, light, water etc.

   - They deserve it. These women truly feel that you are blessed to be with them and for that you must pay the cost to be the boss. And if you're 'paid' they think that you should be spending the money on them. I once gave this girl I was seeing

    Gregory P. Williams

a mink teddy-bear, and she says "you could've just given me the money" I took that furry critter back so fast the fur fell off the doggone thing.

- They say that they want to look good for you so you're in hock for anywhere between $90 to $2,000 (or a rumored $145k for Beyonce's locks) and $80 for her nails plus they'll point out things they've seen that they'd like you to buy; these discussions usually come right after they've whipped that 'thang' on you.

- She's pretty much useless around the house, or should I say your house. She won't cook, clean, or lift a pot unless she thinks there's some gold in it.

- She wants to know how much that pretty car costs or how expensive is that watch. She's trying to figure out if your pockets go down to your ankles or not. So, check yourselves before you wreck yourselves my fellow ShyGuys, she is only there for what she can get and when the money runs out, she'll run out after it. But the gold digger gets a serious nine on the meter!

The Hoochie Mama

I saw a hoochie mama the other day and let me tell you fellas, that skirt was so tight I could read the stretch marks on her behind plus she was sporting some bright red 'hoe shoes' yanno? It's not very hard to get into Ms Lilgirl's panties because she is infatuated with that car of yours and the way you dress. Take her to a swank lounge or club and her eyes get as big as saucers because she thinks you're 'ballin' hard. Yeah, that pretty lil thing has been passed around quite a bit but she means well. Most men would recognize her going a lot easier than they could coming and if the back seat to her car could talk it would ask for a plastic cover. So, if you are looking for a good time the hoochie mama is the place to go. Ms Hoochie Mama gets a real big eight!

The Chicken Headed Skank

Lastly, my favorite girl of all time. The chicken headed skank! This girl is usually more fun than being with three naked sorority sisters in a mud bath. Let us begin with her name- chicken head -this refers to how her head bobs up and down like a chicken's when performing fellacio, and skank speaks to her oh so trampish ways and ooh wee ... I just love her! This girl is so skankish that she will screw anything that moves, which is the reason why plants stop growing when she walks into the room! This girl or woman often seeks attention from outgoing and popular men with lots of status going on.

She usually goes for musicians or cats with money and bling, and she submits to sexual favors with little or no pressure. She changes men as frequently as she changes panties in exclusively sexual relationships and does not discriminate in her choice of men and often picks boys or men from 'around the way'. There is no sexual act that she won't at least try, and she is always ready because she gets turned on just by that very nasty way you look at her. If you can find the right one, she will make for a hellava wife! The chicken headed skank gets a big, whopping ten on the fun meter!

Their personalities
The Flirt

Why does she flirt so much? It could be that she is a retired hoe in transition, and she just can't get fraternizing out of her blood! Nonetheless, the poor baby may be in need of some attention due to her lack of enthusiasm or the quality of attention she craves. By the same token, it could be that the very charming Ms Thang is just unhappy with her station in life. Whatever her motives, that flirty personality and winning smile gets her a seven on the fun meter scale. She is so animated that the air seems to shimmer around her.

 Gregory P. Williams

She makes a boring get together fun and exciting. Let's give the flirt a high five!

The Perpetrator

Individual eyelashes put on: $150. Good weave: $2,000. Nails and toes done in that pretty color you like: $75. Make-up: Lawd only knows cause dayuum, I sho' don't. Nothing about the perpetrator is real except that she is real costly! The funny thing is that with all that stuff put on her she's looking for a real man ... smh. We cannot believe anything that comes out of the perpetrator's mouth as she is phony from head to toe! Look up the word 'fake' and I'll bet you a dollar to a dime that her picture pops up in vivid color. And talk about being untruthful, that girl cannot be believed if she says it's raining out on a damp day! Now for the positive side. If you play it right, you'll find that the 'perp' can be a lot of fun, just don't pull on her weave while having sex cause it might just come off in your hands! I had that happen to me once and it just about scared me half to death. See, it was dark when I felt something in my hand and in the shadows, it looked like a big black spider, needless to say I yelled like a cheerleader at a championship game! Oh, and did I say that she was fraudulent? This lady's fun rating is about a six.

The Party Girl

Whoo hoo! Here comes Ms Party Girl and she is in the mood to dance and otherwise shake what her mama gave her. Not only is she the life of the party but if you and her are somewhere alone you can believe that she is the party. Although, and I must admit, that it does get to be a little tiresome when you call, she's with the girls and when you drop by, she's tired from last night. The party girl is usually attractive from head to toe although she is not too bright cause she's still partying! Now, that girl brings drama to the game cause she is never around when you need her. But still, why don't we give her an eight on the fun meter.

Chatty Cathy

I once dated a Chatty Cathy, and the girl could not stay quiet for two seconds; her mouth was constantly running like an out of tune engine. Lots and lots of random and unnecessary noise. The really crazy thing about her was that she had this extremely high-pitched squeaky voice. Can you just imagine the sounds she would make while making out? Squeak squeak ... Squeak squeak squeak ... Squeeeak ... Now that experience caused me to have nightmares and need medication for a long time.

Most Chatty Cathy's are very opinionated it seems to me. Plus, they seem to always have to be right and they're as bossy as you can get. Now my chatty Cathy turned out to be a skank on steroids and talk about being gossip. But on the other hand, that girl knew what she was doing in the sex department! Chatty Cathy gets a seven on the fun meter and a one on the relationship scale.

The Serial Dater

The definition of a serial dater is someone who engages in the process of systematically dating an obscene amount of people in a short span of time. This lady is the female counterpart to the male playa. This definition encompasses but is not limited to Internet dating, bar dating, long distance flirtations, phone service dating, blind dating, expiration dating, match making, one-night stands, friends with benefits, and personal ad surfing. This girlie is death in high heels. I'm not saying she's a hoe, but she has a lot of men in tow! The serial dater gets a balmy eight on the fun meter.

The Exorcist

What is it that she is exorcising, you ask? Your free will, nights out with the boys, your sinful, wandering, and womanizing mind and ways. She can whip out a verse on the evils of too idle hands and other such matters. Yep, girlie is in it to win it. But she's not all bad as

 Gregory P. Williams

Ms Girly tends to be a sweetheart beneath it all. She just wants what she thinks is best for you.

The exorcist has an organized mind --a place for everything and everything in its place and she wants you to be that way too! Now fellas, I don't know about you, but I tend to leave my favorite writing pen in a couple places around the house. I expect it to be there when I come back for it but Noo. Here she comes moving my stuff and putting it back in its 'place' I guess that's not too high a price to pay for someone so warm and caring. Baby gets a four on the fun meter, but she scores an eleven on the relationship scale when it comes to sticking it out. She's just sweet that way!

The Twerkaholic

We have all seen her in high gear as she walks down the Street causing fender benders and making other women slap their man as he's driving. Look over there, there she is twistin' and werkin' that luscious behind as she strolls down the avenue. She knows all eyes are on her and that the horns being blown are for her benefit. Twerk it girl! And if she screws anywhere near like the way she walks then you may as well clean out your bank account and give her a cashier's check cause dayuum ... You're hooked like a big fish on a five-dollar lure. Ms Twerkaholic gets a big ten on the fun meter!

The Klingon

The most irritating while at the same time the sincerest is the Klingon. She's clinging to your soul, your pocketbook, and she's sucking the very air that you're trying to breathe and ... and ... OMG!! But I digress. My bad. Ms Ferocious will cling on to your dreams, hopes and aspirations while suffocating your soul as you watch in horror as it shrivels and dries before your very eyes! Whew! Just had a flashback ... Okay, I'm back. Now, maybe I'm being a tad too dramatic and harsh toward Ms Clingy but doggone it fellas you know who I'm talking about. Lets give her a three on the fun meter.

Mimi

Mimi's like relationships that give them everything and you nothing. 'It's me me me-let's talk about me- it's all about me-some more about me'. My personal opinion is that Mimi is completely oblivious to everything that isn't her so don't try to impress her as she is too impressed with herself. As far as having fun with her goes she's pretty much alright to take out from time to time but not much more than that because you can't get a word in sideways.

Sex with a Mimi is great because she needs to be able to say that hers is the best 'Thang' this side of the Mississippi River. She is fond of insinuating, "if you get me, you get this hot, sweet and tender Thang". Mimi gets a nine on the fun meter because she is so into herself that you don't have to work too hard.

The Commitmentniac

This lady is committed from that awesome first date when she told you how many kids you would have together and what their names were. Yes, my fellow ShyGuys, run ... Run fast ... Run far. Because she is sizing you up for a wedding suit and the invitations are about to go out and you haven't had much to say about any of it. A word here fellas, if you get one of these you must shake off that shy thing and say no!! Loud and clear. The fun meter is running, and girly gets a seven as she really is a lot of fun ... she just commits too much way too fast.

CHAPTER SIX

Getting Over Shyness- The S.A.M. Approach - Why Being Different is Good

Say Anything Method

Now on to the meat of the guide, how to pull that first conversation out of thin air and get the girl. One night while railroading, me and another rail were standing by the tracks putting in a little work when he told me what he had first said to a girl he was currently dating, he said to her "did it hurt?", she responds "did what hurt?" He follows with "when you fell from heaven". Now I'm not saying that lines don't work because that one is just cute enough to make some girls smile. It's just that they don't work most of the time.

A woman truly dislikes standing on a corner waiting for the light to change, and a fella feeds her one of those sweet candy lines, then she goes across the street to the jazz lounge and hears the exact same thing from someone else. Be original and she will always wonder what's going to drop out of your mouth next!

ShyGuys! This is especially important so check it out. Always be honest in all your dealings with her and you will never have to stumble around with something you might have said. Also, keep your words soft and sweet because you may have to eat them. Which reminds me of the story of the pheasant and the bull.

On a grassy hill stood a bull, and nearby was a tall tree with a pheasant at its base trying desperately to fly up to the lowest branch. The bull seeing this calls out "friend pheasant, friend pheasant what seems to be the problem?" The pheasant, upon hearing him looked up and exclaimed as to how he was trying to fly up to that bottom branch. The bull in his deep voice said, "eat some of my droppings and you'll have the strength to fly there". Well, that bird ate some of the bull's droppings and found that he did indeed have the strength to do it. The next day the pheasant was trying to reach the middle branch and was having a tough time getting there. Upon seeing this the old bull calls out "friend pheasant, friend pheasant eat more of my droppings, and you'll have the strength to fly farther". Well, that old bird dropped down to the ground and ate more of the bull's droppings then flew right up to that middle branch. Now, the next day that pheasant was trying to get to the highest branch of the tree when the bull calls out "friend pheasant ..." And down that bird drops and eats an entire pile of the Bulls droppings then sprang into the air, flying to the highest branch, and sat proudly.

One day the farmer comes by and seeing that old bird preening and strutting, raises his shotgun and blows him straight out of that tree. And the moral of this story? bullshit might get you to the top, but it won't keep you there. Always remember my fellow ShyGuys, keep it real when you can't keep it right! Talk to her, not at her -let your lips be silent for a moment and really hear and respond to her.

Listen to what she is saying. Don't think about the next thing you're going to say. A lot of us have that problem that arises whenever we talk to a girl. We talk about ourselves out of sheer nervousness and believing we have nothing else to say. I will talk to a woman by letting her speak as much as she wants to, interjecting a comment every now and then, yep ... That's right .... uh huh. At the end of the conversation don't be too surprised when she says, "I had a really nice time talking to you, you're quite the conversationalist!" Or something along those

     Gregory P. Williams

lines. Let your lips stop the talking and let hers do the walking and really hear what she's saying. You'll find that she's given you lots of things that are important to her to talk about. I use what I like to call the S.A.M. approach. It's the 'Say Anything Method'. When I tell you to say anything that's just what I mean, just keep it suited to the type of girl you're talking to.

Here is a scenario: you walk up to a woman you find attractive, ask her something completely unglued like "did you see that purple duck that just when that way?" Now pay close attention to her face and especially her eyes because they're going through a lot of changes right now -it's really pretty fun to watch - she'll go everywhere from 'is this guy hinged right' to 'OMG!' and every place in between. She's trying to figure if you are sane, strange, funny etc. While she's going through her personal crisis, stick out your hand out and introduce yourself. You are holding her hand now and all it took from seeing Ms cutie to knowing her name and having her hand in yours took about thirty seconds. How's that for speed dating?

The Say Anything Method is at the core of this manual. When first we approach Ms Gotta Have Her, S.A.M. is where we begin to count down those first thirty seconds. You may be wondering at this point just what it is you say to her. Let me step outside for just a minute and see what is there to talk about. Okay, I'm back. You could walk up to Ms Beautiful Mint Julep and say "if you were a flower, which one would you be?" I'll bet she hasn't heard that too often. Something that small will catch her completely off guard because when she sees you walking toward her, she is expecting some tired and worn-out line. Alternatively, you could comment on her hair with something like "I like the way your hair frames your face" it's those simple little things that will attract her attention. There is really no mystery involved. On the other hand, you could go for the gusto and say, "if we could bottle that walk of yours, we'd get Rich" What we are looking for here is something to break the ice, something that will pull a conversation out of thin air. Once you have put a smile on that lovely face of hers, queen-check as they say in chess parlance.

Okay so you think you like her but is it because you really like her or because it's expected that a man should have a woman? The first thing you must decide is why you want her. If you just want to have sex with her there are girls out there for that. Moreover, if you want a wife or a girlfriend there are things you need to know about them also. First off you need to understand that a female wants what she thinks she can't have, so if you're easy ... Well, there you go.

Negativity has no place in our lives fellas so shake that off. The conversation is going smooth and mellow like a smoke-filled jazz lounge on the coast when you say, "don't you just hate the traffic around here at 5 o'clock?" You just threw the word hate out there and her subconscious is busy as a little bee imagining all the pictures that word calls forth. Try not to use the word never too often either, as in 'I never do this, or I never do that' it marks you as someone who isn't flexible and ready to go with the flow at a moment's notice. No spontaneity.

Like my sainted and departed grandmother used to say, "if you can't say anything positive then don't say anything at all!" Look deeply into Ms Lovely's eyes and see if you can find truth there because it certainly is true that the eyes are the Windows into the soul. A moment about those wandering and roaming eyes of yours; stop looking at those tig 'ol bitties. Stop it! Stop it! Stop it! You'll miss what she's trying to say to you, and she'll figure all you want is sex, so look thoughtfully into her eyes when speaking to her.

Doesn't it just irk you when someone's eyes keep darting around instead of being focused on you? I know it bothers me. Besides ShyGuys, it is not a sign of a dominant personality. Passive/submissive or sneaky people tend not to look into the other person's eyes.

So, what is there to talk about out of the blue? Just look around and you will find thousands of things to talk about ... The sky, nature or just a thought you are having. This is where the S.A.M approach comes in handy because it allows you to say whatever. Walk up to the pretty girl and tell her how you wish you were that lovely dress she is

 Gregory P. Williams

wearing or something as important to her as the way she styles her hair ... Love the shoes too sweetie.

Let me just stop for a moment and talk about compliments, don't lavish them on her because she will think you weak and hungry. Just a 'love the purse' is enough. If you look around and talk about everything you see, eventually you will run across something that will make her eyes light up. They like compliments but keep it to a minimum (not her looks). Her dress etc. her smile, her weave, oops I mean hair.

Relax. Relate. Respond! A lady friend of mine says that.

I could write an entire chapter on body language, and how it affects the opposite sex. You can tell just how much a woman likes you by how often they touch you or allow you to touch them. Body language conveys all types of emotions from anger to love to sex. Check out a couple sometime and see how often she touches or doesn't touch his hand or some other body part while talking or just sitting there.

Always stand tall, it's a sign of confidence. I'm only five foot ten but people often mistake me for being six foot or so because of how I carry myself, head up and shoulders squared with my feet spread apart about as wide as my shoulders. Was that Shakespeare who said, "all the worlds a stage and the people in it merely players"? From the moment you walk out of the house to the time you return home, you are on stage so walk like you know where you're going with an easy smile on your face. Well, maybe not the smile all the time.

I remember once while living in Washington DC, I was on a bus thinking about the highways and by-ways of life and not really giving a thought about anything in particular when I heard this voice "hey!" I didn't pay any attention to it because I was wandering around GregoryLand where the people are always nice, and the weather is always fine when I heard that voice again "hey!" I looked up and there was this fella staring at me and he said angrily "what are you smiling about? "I replied, "I haven't had to knock anyone out today, so I'm feeling really good about myself" he left me alone. I have a pleasant look on my face most of the time because I know I'm on the big screen and there's no telling who's looking.

Okay, you've found Ms Cutie Pie and you're dating. Don't get too serious too soon. Don't be a Commitmentniac, it will scare her off. Try to keep everything light and friendly. I know I keep saying this but it's important: do not act hungry! That will throw her off too. Which reminds me of this girl I once met on a train. I started talking about anything and everything (SAM) got her attention, and fellas let me tell you I was as smooth as an eight ball and baby was feeling my flow. Then over the next few days I screwed it up by becoming serious way too soon. Not long after that was the last time I saw her. Do not fall into this trap.

Here you are having a pleasant conversation when suddenly, she goes dead silent. Her facial expression changes and she remembers that she has something to do. You've just screwed up! And you don't know what happened, so immediately jump to her favorite subject and wait for her face and shoulders to relax. You can always use that old standby and say something funny or simply ask her what's wrong.

Now I'm not anywhere near perfect and find myself having screwed up conversationally every now and then. So, what I do is see if she wants to go to dinner and a movie or if the weather is right a drive to the coast with a picnic basket. However you do it, turn her attention to something pleasant and/or romantic.

Treat her like a person and not an object -I know I keep saying this also but it is true that if you put her up on a pedestal she'll pee down in your face. But hey, maybe you like water sports. Keep her attention focused on you, she probably isn't all that anyway. When she sticks her nose in the air give her a reality check.

ShyGuys, you must understand that she's just like you and me with her own likes and dislikes. She gets cold, she gets hot and when a bee stings her, she'll say ouch. She is just a girl... No big deal. We

 Gregory P. Williams

ShyGuys need to learn how to talk with a girl not just talk at her. Just walk up to her and ask if she would like to have dinner and a movie. Easy as that. The worst that she can do is say no. Then you say "Ok, get out of line miss next!"

Some guys like to hide behind the facade of a rap star, hip-hopster type. I mean if that's who you are then go on with ya bad self ... I'm not a hater, I'm a congradulater. I'm not pointing any fingers but yeah, I'm talking to you. Every time I turn around, I have to hear bitch this and bitch that. You do know that when the glitter and gold run out, they'll run out right after it right? Vulgarity is not essential or necessary in the process of getting a girl. Don't get me wrong there are a whole lot of women out there who only respect the rap star, hip-Hopster type, so throw some SAM at them leaving them bedazzled, confused, and befuddled.

Always be a gentleman but be aware that most women mistake kindness for weakness. Gentleman is spelled: Gentle Man ... always be a Gentleman until it's time not to be. Remember that saying "good guys finish last?" It's true. We ShyGuys are basically good guys by nature, so we have to keep a firm hand and let Ms Want To Take Control know that we are not suckers. How do we do this you ask? You do it by taking the lead. Someone has to drive the car so it may as well be you seeing as you already know which direction you want things to go. Do not be afraid to correct her when she's wrong, she expects the man to do that.

You don't have to know everything about everything (don't try to impress her). If you know how to type don't tell her, just start typing ... If you know how to work on a car don't tell her, when the time comes just start working on it. Show her what you know, do not just tell her. If you always tell her what you know she'll think you're a know it all but if you show her, she'll be impressed. (That is if you really do know a lot). She will also think you're insecure if you're a know it all. Be careful when using the words 'I know'. When dealing with an 'I know' type I'll sometimes say something totally bizarre like "I was reading in the paper today that Jupiter is in a singular juxtaposition to Mars" just to hear them say "I know" then listen as they go on to explain this and other such celestial phenomena. I know I shouldn't do that but sometimes I just can't resist.

Just like we ShyGuys or anyone else for that matter don't like to be stood up? Well fellas, she doesn't like it either so build a reputation of keeping your word. We have to earn her trust and we do this in small ways like being on time and picking her up when we say we will - do what you say you're going to do. So be sure not to say or do anything you don't really mean because baby is over there keeping score on what you do and don't do. Besides, be on time enough times and she might get the hint and be on time herself.

I've said it before, and I will say it again - know when to shut it up! If she's still talking, then you need to hush your mouth because she just might be saying something you need to hear. I know there've been times early on when I would be close to hitting a home run then I started running my mouth and there my opportunity went straight out the door. I had to learn how to relax and just let it flow naturally. Sometimes we work excessively hard trying to get the girl, not knowing that all the while the girl is trying to get you too. So don't screw it up, just screw it shut! Practice: go somewhere quiet and close your eyes. Picture a beautiful woman in your mind's eye and see yourself walking up and talking to her. Do this picturing different women.

Chapter Seven

Getting Girls is Like Fishing- You Just Have to Have the Right Bait for the Species You Want

Once you have decided which type of girl you want you then have to determine what type of bait to use in order to get and keep her attention. Here are a few of the baits I personally use:

- For the good girl you don't want to overdress. I've found that being too dressy for some reason throws them off, so I go for the jeans and cowboy boot look.
- The shy girl seems to like me when I'm casually dressed. With them, I have discovered that they crave to hear new and exciting things.

Now for the hood rat. For this girl I always dress really clean and carry what used to be called a Mexican bankroll and for those of you that don't know, a Mexican bankroll is a few hundred-dollar bills on top of a couple of 50s surrounding a bunch of ones, she'll think you're Ballin real hard.

One word for the gold digger ... Bling ... Plus a car and a house. That's what lures her in. A car is all you need to catch a hoochie mama as she is used to screwing in the back seat For the chicken headed skank you need a real nasty vocabulary and nice places to take her. You never get a second chance to make a first impression so always be at the top your game. You have to put your best face on when you walk out that front door because you never know when or where that love light is going to show up.

I keep my breath fresh and wear cologne that's a real pantie dropper. Some type of lip balm or the like is a good thing because you want your lips to look kissable. No woman wants to press her sweet lips against crusty chapped ones. Find a style that fits you and try not to look like anyone else. I like slacks, boots, and Stetson hats, that style fits my personality.

Charm. Charm. Charm. I can't say enough about it. We'll discuss how to be charming a little later on, so I won't get into it too deeply here. Just remember charm plus personality equals big returns. Personality to me is that vibrant quality to your voice, that swag when you walk and that pleasant look on your face. I once knew a fella who looked like Baby Milo from planet of the apes, but he had the most beautiful girl. I scratched my head then one day I decided to ask him. He said one word then calmly walked away "charm".

How many times have we seen a man with a real pretty girl on his arm and wonder 'just how did he get her?' Following this guide will give you everything you need to catch that trophy you've always wanted. Remember fellas, you don't need that bling if you've got that zing! (But it helps).

We've come far enough in the program to start doing a little personal maintenance. I firmly believe that all romantic situations arise from a smile. I see those rappers frowning and think to myself "if it weren't for the money, homie would be straight out of luck". I know there are females out there who like that kinda thing but that's

          Gregory P. Williams

not the type of woman I personally want. Practice smiling, it gives your face a calm and relaxed glow.

About teeth- if yours are not in the best shape, go to the dentist and that'll be the best money you ever spent. The dentist and Barber are worth every cent. If you can't afford the dentist, then buy some of those teeth whiteners to hold you in the meantime in between time.

Yanno, some guys will stand in the mirror for hours trying to get every hair in place. I'm sometimes guilty of that myself then I have to step back and say, 'perfection is not attainable, no matter how hard I might try'. So I just do the best that I can. An older man told me all that was not even necessary. See, it's your attitude that makes you look good and not particularly what you see in the mirror although it does help.

I remember years ago standing at the front desk of this company in Silicon Valley, when this salesman walked in all dressed and pressed, not a single hair out of place. The girl walked up to her side of the desk, looked at him and busted out laughing. I thought 'how rude' then she said "Sir, you have a worm in your hair" I looked and sure as honey is sweet there was this little green worm inching its way across his head. He brushed his hair and the worm fell out, but then his hair was all jacked up and the girl started laughing harder. When he walked in, he had this swagger about him, now his head was hanging, and he looked completely defeated. The point is if he really had swagger and attitude, he could've played his way out of that and kept it moving instead of having his day ruined.

My fellow ShyGuys, you must get yourself a car if you don't get anything else because plain and simple it's hard for Ms Shawty to ride on your bike in a short skirt so make it a priority. With a car you can expand your hunting grounds so instead of fishing for the girls nearby you can go to another small town or big city.

Besides, you need to be able to take her places like dinner or a movie. Then there are all the things you can do while driving down the street with her. Fellas, there's nothing finer than pulling over to the side of the road in some secluded place then you and her get your swerve on!

ShyGuys, put those video games down and keep that money you spend on them in your pocket to take that fine thing out to places she likes. Maybe theme parks, the lake or some beach somewhere quiet and secluded. Whatever it is, you'll need money to do that. Don't ever think that dating or sex is free or cheap it isn't. Yes fellas, she'll make you pay for it in some way, form, or fashion. Whether spending money on hotels, dinners, flowers and candy or gas for your car in order to get to her, it's gonna cost you so you're going to need every dime!

Fish get used to the same old lure, so you must change up from time to time. The same is true with dating, women get used to hearing the same old lines or doing the same old things. Change the game up and do things she probably has never done before -keep it fresh and exciting -I remember one time me and this girl took a trip up to the mountains where I took her to a beautiful waterfall that I knew of. We climbed up the rocks and there behind the fall was a ledge big enough for two people and it was there that we had some of the best lovin we ever had. That was something she'd never done before, and it excited her to the nth degree. Use your imagination and come up with different things for you and her to do.

While we're on the subject of bait, here's a lure that I've used with a great deal of success in the past. Take a kid somewhere women congregate like the park, malls and playgrounds etc. did I just hear someone say "what the ...?" Yep, a kid. If you're already a father all the better if not, borrow one from a sibling, relative or friend. Women will view you as responsible, likable, and fatherly. It'll bring out their maternal instincts.

Not long ago I took my four-year-old granddaughter to the park and women surrounded me saying things like "oh, what a beautiful child" and "you don't see many men taking time with the kids" and these were young women hitting on me. Boy oh boy, had I been single

    Gregory P. Williams

I would've come home with three or four phone numbers! It never hurts to know a joke or two; my motto is 'always keep 'em laughin'. I'll have her cracking up all the while pulling her panties off. Always keep it light and easy going, if you start getting really deep and real serious, she'll just cut and run away.

By the way, did you hear the one about the big fish? Well, these two guys were fishing and talking about women as men do when one of them said "I pulled a fish out of the lake at this very spot, it was so big the water level dropped by two inches". The other guy says, "I was fishing this very spot too and pulled out a lantern, funny thing was it was still lit". The first guy says, "stop lying, you know you didn't pull out a lit lantern". Guy replies "if you put your fish back, I'll blow out my lantern!"

Just like something that shines will make a fish bite, it holds true that something shiny will make a female bite too. I know this sounds superficial and shallow but hey, women are a different species all together and you have to use the materials at hand. Be sure to wear something shiny in a conspicuous place where she is sure to see it. First, she'll ask you about it then her eyes will unconsciously follow its every movement, hypnotizing her into a state of total compliance!

Or take your remote-controlled car and send it in her direction with a note attached! Doing different things like that will catch her attention. I would send a note asking for her name and number and more times than not I'd get a positive response if nothing more than a knowing smile inviting me to come over for some conversation and fun. So you see, there are all kinds of bait out there, it's only limited by your imagination. Just be sure to keep it original.

Chapter Eight

Don't Fish the Same River or Lake, Try different Waters

With the world becoming smaller and smaller because of advancements in communications, it is much easier to contact a larger number and variety of women from differing backgrounds. In other words, there are plenty of fish in the sea! So don't be afraid of rejection because for every one girl who'll reject you there are literally thousands of girls out there looking for someone just like you and all you have to do is step up and reach out your hand.

Online Dating / Chat

Online dating can be lots of fun as well as profitable as it were. There's the mystery of who that person behind the keyboard really is. The thing about online dating is that the other person can be anyone she wants to be and since she probably thinks you'll never meet in person she may present herself as being the Queen of the Americas! Lots of people out there are perpetrating some seriously fraudulent behavior.

More than once I've gotten close to a girl online, saw her picture and thought it was all good then when I actually saw her, I was like "woman, why did you lie to me?" Because she looked nothing like her picture. She said that she wanted me to like her for her, which is all good, but I would rather and very shallowly I admit, date a woman I find attractive.

After a couple times or so of that I bought myself a web cam so I could actually see her as we chatted. But be careful here ShyGuys because there are some not so shy guys out there impersonating women. I would tell them how I feel then say "stop your grinnin' and drop your linen" so I can see what 'cha got! If they don't, I would just figure they're perpetrating fraud and keep it moving.

Bookstores

Bookstores are a great place to find women. If they had a man nine times out of ten, they probably wouldn't be there alone. She's reading so that means she is at least intelligent enough to do that. Walk over and introduce yourself then ask her what's a good book to read and from that we can gather two things:

1. how her mind works depending on what she's reading and suggests -sci-fi, romance, adventure and,
2. just how charming and pleasing is her personality. Note that at the same time she's measuring you up too.

From there on just be your charming self and talk to her as if you've known her forever, like an old and dear friend. (See the section on charm). By the time she's finished talking, you can hand her your card and take hers if she has one. Side note here, there are places online that will give you free basic cards. I like to call them social cards as opposed to business cards. I keep two sets, one for business and the other for socializing. Each has its own pertinent information.

Church

When you start wondering where all the really pretty women are at, look toward the church. These women usually go to work then back home. You rarely see them unless some special event is in town like an art show or fashion show. They're mostly in church looking for two things, salvation, and a man! A lot of the time they've been held back sexually by their parents and the church's teachings, so they're chomping at the bit looking for some excitement in their otherwise mostly dull lives. Well, let me change that just a bit because I've known some church girls who party hardy on Friday and Saturday then pray for forgiveness on Sunday!

The House Party

House parties are another place to go because you probably know the people throwing the party and they know most of the people who show up. They can introduce you around. Most of the girls at house parties pretty much plan on getting laid that night so be charming, funny, and dressed to impress! The music is blaring, and the alcohol is flowing, the girls are getting seriously lit and ready to dance and have fun.

The Club

"The roof, the roof, the roof is on fire!" (Oops telling my age). I don't do the club scene much anymore but when I did, it was an all-night affair. I was up in this club in the San Francisco Bay Area when there was a tap on my back. I turned around to see the prettiest girl standing there with tears in her eyes she said, "it's my birthday" and just like that it was on. I kinda like the wall flowers standing and sitting around the joint just waiting for someone to come over and take their hand. You have wall flowers, dancers, and drinkers ... Take your pick. The club gets a big high five for available females.

There are so many ponds to fish in that I don't know how many to mention. The library and social events. Go to the grocery store and act helpless by asking for help, as you don't know what to get. The County fair is also the place to go with everyone having fun. And this may sound terrible, but the courthouse is an excellent place because baby's man just went to jail, she's single for now, she has tears in her eyes and she's vulnerable.

 Gregory P. Williams

The Mall

The malls are rich with females either alone or in groups. I'll go to the jewelry stores so the ladies say 'Wonder what he could buy me'. More than once I've been standing in front of the store when Ms. buy me that ring commented on my apparent good taste in jewelry and let me tell you I could see money signs light up in her eyes... cha Ching!

I would then say something like "have you had lunch yet?" She would give me the answer I was waiting for and off we would go to some nice eatery then take a ride up to the lake enjoying the afternoon and each other's company. By the same token, I'd go to the women's department at various stores and if I'm looking for a hood rat, I'll go to a low end place and when I'm on the prowl for something different, I'll go to an upscale spot and ease myself on over to the big ticket items. That way I know the girl has her own loot and won't be reaching her hand out for mine!

Victoria's Secret or Places Like That

I Just love Victoria's secret or the like because when you meet a woman there you have an idea of what she's wearing under that skirt and Ms Freaky is freaky as she can be, but not many people know that because her exterior is so lady like. Yep fellas, a lady in the streets and a freak in the sheets. She may be wearing a silk thong with a bra that has holes for the nipples to poke out. Now there she goes over to the perfumed soap areas, so you know what to buy her when the time comes. If you're in there she figures you there to buy your lady friend or wife something sexy and some smell good.

We know that women want what another woman has so, if she thinks you're single she will think 'if another woman doesn't want him, then why should I?' Moreover, if you're looking at some really interesting item, say a see-through nightie with matching crotchless panties, the girl now knows what you like. So, if she likes men who just love freaky lingerie, well there you are!

Motorcycle Club Event (girls are everywhere)

Now if you can't catch a woman at a motorcycle club event then something is seriously wrong with you, and I can't help ya! See, they're there to get their party on and get laid. All you have to do is not screw it up! Next to a cruise ship, this is about the easiest place to find women.

I was at one such event when this pretty girl walked past me wearing a see-through dress and stiletto's, that was all. All I had to do was to reach out my hand and say "hello, hey girl can I get you a drink? Oh, and by the way, I'm Gregory P". She introduced herself and the party was on and crackin' as they say. She was already in the mood to say yes to someone, all I had to do was not give her a reason to say no!

Weddings

Weddings are an excellent source for females. I don't know if you've noticed but weddings and the after party are full of sexy and hot girls and women just looking for someone to marry someday. The champagne and wine is flowing like a fountain and love is in the air. A slow jam is playing, and everyone is in the mood, "hey girl, care to dance?" and just like that, you're holding someone you find attractive in your arms, and she is gently swaying her body against yours. The thing is, it is a place full of women just like her so you can take your pick.

Funerals

This is not a Dead Subject (ok, bad dead pun!) The women are friendly and need some laughter or someone to just talk quietly with. Yanno, the more I think about this particular topic the more I feel like I'm taking advantage of someone during their time of vulnerability. Then I say to myself "self, you mean the way they'll take advantage of you if you give them a running start?" Okay fellas, I was having a moment there, but it's passed and I feel great! She's leaning gently against my chest and then she looks up into my eyes with her mist filled ones and I whisper into her ear, reassuring her. Doggone Gregory that sounds cold. Fellas, forget I even mentioned this one.

Baby Showers

Baby showers ... oh yeah! Maternal instincts are running rampant today because all of these girls want to be married and pregnant. Be careful here because you could end up hooked up for a very long time. These girls are on the prowl for a single man just like you! Speaking of which, some of those pregnant girls are currently single because instead of being with one of us (the good guys), they opted for the playa/jock type as they usually do and now, he's gone.

Most of the women there are single although there are quite a few married ones in the room too. All you have to do is mingle, being your charming and friendly self. You'll end up with a phone number or two, that is if you can get in! The ones without kids are thinking that they may want one someday too and that means sex is in the back of their minds somewhere although she's probably unaware of it

Hardware Stores or Some Other DIY (Do It Yourself) Store

Lots of single ladies can be found in home improvement stores. And they just love a man who can fix and build things. Yes people, Ms Babydoll is single and has lots of things that need repair. Maybe she is decorating and changing things around a bit. She wants new faucets in the bathroom and needs to hang some artwork on the walls, so she needs picture hangers and things like that.

She wants new doorknobs to put on all the doors plus her gazebo out back and spa need some repair not to mention her car could use a little help too. As she walks around the store, she sees you standing close by (that's because you positioned yourself there), you ask a question or two about something she is trying to do, about what project she is currently working on which, by the way, is a good icebreaker.

You have your cards with you (like American Express, never leave home without them), so you give her one and let her know that if she needs help or advice on a particular project, you're just a phone call away! That's called setting a trap. Then you sit back and see if she walks into it.

Gregory P. Williams

CHAPTER NINE

How to Be Charming

Charm is the art of having an attractive personality. This characteristic can be achieved only over a period of time. While everyone is born with differing amounts of natural charm, much can be acquired and honed through practice and patience. As with dancing, the more you practice the better you will become.

The steps to being charmingly charming:

1. Be genuinely interested in people- you don't have to love everyone, but you should be curious or fascinated by people in some way. If you're empathic, you're interested in how people feel. On the other hand, you could be interested in how people work (psychology), or what people know (if you're in Avid learner}. Learn how to ask questions based on your interests while being polite (i.e., without prying} and others will feel they are interesting.

2. Remember people's names when you meet them for the first time -this takes an enormous amount of effort for most people. When introducing yourself, repeating the person's name will help you remember it. For example, "hi Laura, I'm Gregory". Follow through with small talk and use the person's name during your conversation. Repeat it once more when you say goodbye. Repeating someone's name is not just about helping you to remember that person. The more often you say

someone's name, the more that person will feel that you like them and the greater the chance they'll warm up to you.

3. Assume rapport -this simply means talking to a stranger or newly met acquaintance in a very friendly manner, as if the person is a long-lost friend or relative. This helps break down an initial awkwardness and speeds up the warm-up process when meeting new people. Soon, people will feel more welcome and comfortable around you. Kindness coupled with respect makes others feel as if they are loved and cared for. This is a powerful tool during interactions.

4. Smile with your eyes -scientists have pinpointed more than fifty types of smiles, and research suggests that the sincerest smile of all is the Duchenne smile -a smile that pushes up into the eyes. The reason it's more genuine is because the muscles needed to smile with our eyes is involuntary; they only become engaged in an authentic smile, not in just a courtesy smile.

5. Consider topics that interest those around you, even if you are not so keen on them -if you're in a sporty crowd, talk about last night's game or the meteoric rise of a new team. If you're with a group of hobbyists, ask about their hobbies and make pertinent remarks related to fishing, knitting, mountain climbing, movies, etc. Nobody expects you to be an expert. Sometimes you can create a good rapport just by asking questions, and not caring if you seem naive. There are people who like talking about and explaining their interests and will like you for listening. It is your level of interest and willingness to engage in topics that makes you an interesting person to be around. Exercise an open mind. Let others do the explaining. If someone mistakenly thinks you know more about the topic than you actually do, be genuine and simply say that your knowledge is limited but that you're hoping to learn more about it. Control your tone of voice -the tone of your voice is crucial. Voice should be gentle and peaceful. Articulate, speak clearly, and project your voice. When you

   Gregory P. Williams

say, "You look nice today" it should be in the exact same tone that you would use to say, "it's a nice day". Any variation from your normal tone will arouse suspicion about your sincerity. Practice giving compliments to a recorder and play it back. Does it sound sincere? Practice until you get it right!

6. Watch the way you phrase things -be mature and have a touch of wise, polite language. Don't you find people that say "hello" much more charming than people that mutter "sup"? Here's another example: change "it's none of his beeswax!" To "it shouldn't be any of his concern". Of course, don't overdo it, but try to be polite and turn every negative into a positive. It will really give you charm.

7. Issue compliments generously; this especially raises other's self-esteem - pick out something that you appreciate in any situation and verbally express that appreciation. If you like something or someone, find a creative way to say it and say it at once. If you wait too long, it may be viewed as insincere and badly timed, especially if others have beaten you to it. Because you waited you are most likely not confident in saying what you thought; waiting will result in a less than enthusiastic presentation. If you notice that someone is putting a lot of effort into something, compliment him or her even if you feel that there is room for improvement. If you notice that someone has changed something about themselves (haircut, manner of dress, etc.) notice it and point out something you like about it. If you're asked directly, be charming and deflect the question with a very general compliment.

8. Be gracious in accepting compliments -get out of the habit of assuming that a compliment is being given without genuine intent. Even when someone makes a compliment out of contempt, there is always a germ of jealous truth hiding in his or her own heart. Be effusive in accepting compliments. Go beyond a mere "thank you" and make it a "I'm glad you like it", or "it is so kind of you to have noticed" these are compliments in return. Avoid backhanding a compliment...

There is nothing worse to a person complimenting than to receive the response "oh well, I wish I was as (fill in the blank) as you in that situation" this is tantamount to saying "no, I am not what you are saying I am; your judgment is wrong.

9. Praise others instead of gossiping -if you're speaking with someone or talking in a group of people, and up pops the subject of another person in a positive or negative way, be the one to mention something you like about that person. Kind hearsay is the most powerful tool in gaining charm because it is always viewed as 100% sincere. It has the added benefit of creating trust in you. The idea will spread that you will never have a bad word to say about anyone. Everyone will know that his or her reputation is safe with you.

10. Sometimes being charming is about simply being a good listener - charm isn't always an outward expression, but an inward one too. Engage the other person to talk more about himself or herself, about something that they like, something they're passionate about, about themselves. This makes the other person more comfortable to share and express himself or herself with you.

11. A few tips:

    - Behave honestly; being honest will add points in front of others.
    - Do not avoid eye contact. Look into their eyes when you talk to them.
    - Cursing is something to avoid; it puts a lot of people off and won't make you seem like a charming person.
    - Add a bit of humor to your conversation but keep it civil.
    - Smile at people you meet. Also, when you greet someone make them feel they are the most important person to you. They will respond more nicely and always know what a great person you are.

     Gregory P. Williams

- The degree of charm that you possess depends on the creativity of your praise. Say something that is not immediately obvious and say it in a poetic way. It's good to have premeditated compliments and phrases but the most charming people are able to invent them on the spot. This way, you can be sure that you are not repeating it. If you can't think of anything to say, bring up a current event that is interesting.
- Empathy is at the core of charm. If you can't tell what makes people happy or unhappy, you have no way to assess whether you are saying the right or wrong thing.
- Put some humor in the things you say. Most girls love a guy who can make them laugh.
- Improve your posture. Throw those shoulders back and let them drop (relax). When you walk, imagine you're crossing a finish line; the first part of your body to cross the line would be your torso not your head. If you have poor posture, your head will be pushed forward, which makes you seem timid and insecure. If forcing good posture doesn't look right, strengthen your muscles. These would include your upper back (traps and lats), shoulders and chest. Your neck will fall into place and your posture will be perfect naturally.
- Do not assume that you have the right to include yourself in a conversation that is not addressed to you, or you know nothing about. Expressing your opinion when it hasn't been asked for just demonstrates arrogance and immaturity.
- Be yourself and try adding your personality to the conversation but not just talk about yourself. That would make you seem egocentric and uninterested in the other person's feelings.

- Try standing to the right of a person when you talk to them. Try things you normally wouldn't do.

Warnings

- Don't confuse being charming with being a people pleaser.
- Something may be obvious to you but not so simple to others. Understand that and help them out.
- Every so often, you will have no choice but to express an opinion that few others hold. That is fine. Consider expressing it in a humorous way. Humor is the spoonful of sugar that helps the medicine go down.

Gregory P. Williams

CHAPTER TEN

A Little Swagger Doesn't Hurt

Don't slouch because it makes you look like a potato bug. Swagger or swag as they say, is that purposeful walk and way of talking. Looking people in the eye exudes confidence! People often ask me how did I develop my walk - my walk? - Don't have a clue fellas, but I've had women tell me that I should open a school and teach men how to carry themselves. Well ShyGuys, I don't know about all that but what I do know is that mom made me balance a big dictionary on my head when I was a kid. It taught me to stand up straight and not to slouch, maybe that's what they mean.

What I will say is that how you stand says a lot about you. If your head is hung down you tend to look insecure and weak, at least in my humble opinion and don't get me started on sagging your pants until your ass shows (but if that's how you roll go for it). Stand tall my fellow ShyGuys, you're a force to be reckoned with! Here's where we learn to have some swagger in our mannerisms fellas and walk as if we have somewhere to be, with a purpose. In other words, I been where I been, and I'll be where I'm goin'.

Often-times others will mistake my confidence for arrogance or cockiness when in reality all it is, is my belief that I am no better and no worse than anyone else. It is the belief that I really am an individual with my own thoughts and desires.

Having that sense of who you are will propel you to heights you never knew existed. When you're centered, there is absolutely nothing you can't do. Let me share something I read many years ago: Whatever The mind of man can Conceive and Believe It can Achieve. If you truly make yourself believe you're that charming, romantic, and caring man then you can attain that. Believe in yourself and others will follow.

Knowledge doesn't necessarily come from academic pursuits, some of us just have a natural ability to learn merely from reading a book, others will have to study a bit but the point I'm trying to make is that the more you know then the better you can respond in differing situations. There are two books that I highly recommend you read. Napoleon Hill's 'Think and Grow Rich' and Maxwell Maltz's 'Psycho Cybernetics'.

You're you, you're singular and needed in this world. You have something to contribute and although you may not know what that is at this moment don't worry, in time it'll come to you. Learn to be comfortable in your own skin and not try to be someone else. Can you imagine a bear trying to be a mountain lion? Won't work. They're who and what they are. What you must realize is that you're pretty much stuck with you although you don't have to be stuck with how you carry yourself. You can learn and develop different traits and habits.

Fellas, relax she's just a girl right? Right. Uptight makes you look and act nervous. The funny thing about a female is that she's human with human needs, wants and desires -just like you -she has a wide range of feelings from totally happy to pitifully sad and everything in between -just like you. Yep, Ms Girlie Girl has her own thoughts believe it or not (although sometimes you have to wonder) thoughts of doing and being -just like you.

Are you starting to see a pattern here? ShyGuys, she is just like us except that she is ruled by her emotions while we're led by logic (supposed to be anyway). So, when you run across Ms All You Want

 Gregory P. Williams

don't be afraid of her. She's probably just as afraid of you for the very same reasons.

I'm from the old school that says when you greet someone you stand up and shake hands. Lots of times I'll introduce myself and homie would just sit there apparently happy to have me stand over him - that puts me in a dominant position -I call what they do weak character. Stand up and look into their eyes when you greet them, it'll make them respect you.

Like I said before you never get a second chance to make a first impression so keep your game tight! Your new demeanor will likely have people looking at you differently, they'll wonder why they never noticed just how charming you truly are.

With a pretty woman by your side other women will look at and flirt with you. Her curiosity is piqued and she's wondering 'what does he have' and 'why's she with him'. Happens all the time so be aware and don't blow your date by flirting back. Being casually charming as always will now do two things; first of all, your date is going look at you with admiration and secondly, if the other woman is your waitress, you'll get excellent service!

I have an attractive wife who dresses with her own personal style and flair and let me tell you fellas, when we step out 'the girls, the girls, they love me!' I get a serious kick out of them trying to quietly slide me their number.

Being ShyGuys, we are almost to a man, naturally soft spoken around women and that can prove to be a disability. I've found that most women prefer a man with a commanding voice, whispering has its place like when you're whispering those sugar sweet things into her ear. Women tend to like men with strong voices -not loud -strong. There's a difference fellas.

Speak as if what you're saying is the most important message this world can have. Try to learn how to speak from your diaphragm, make your voice come from deep within your chest. I know it sounds difficult if not downright impossible, but trust me guys it can be done. I've trained my voice to do just that, and the responses are great "ooh, I just love your voice" and things like that. PRACTICE .. PRACTICE .. PRACTICE!

Practice ... As we talked about earlier, getting women is a numbers game. The more women you talk to the better your chance of success. So try this. Go someplace where there are lots of women; places like malls, swap meets, movie theaters, etc. Walk up to a woman you find attractive and say this: "hello, I'm (insert your name) and I'm a ShyGuy learning to be a social butterfly" (stick out your hand for her to shake, now you're holding hands). I would then say to her, "in order to achieve that I have to walk up to an attractive woman I don't know and start a conversation out of the blue. How am I doing so far?" (Smile and wink sweetly). And that was honest and original, you didn't have to come up with a 'line'. Now, she'll either laugh, smile, frown, walk away, whatever. It doesn't matter what her response. What matters is that you did it! Now repeat that every chance you get, and you'll find yourself being more and more at ease doing it. Soon it'll become second nature, and you won't about it at all.

Most of you have probably heard the story of the old bull and the young bull. Two Bulls were standing on top of a grassy knoll looking down at all the pretty cows just mulling around when the young bull said, "lets run down there and screw one", to which the old bull replied, "lets walk down and screw them all!"

So, what do you do now that you have Ms Girlie Girls number? Nothing! That's right don't run in there calling every day because you'll just scare her off! girl just might figure you for a stalker. Give it two or three days, that's just about enough time to let her know you're interested but that you're not a bug a boo yanno? It also gives her enough time to think about you too.

            Gregory P. Williams

CHAPTER ELEVEN

What to do Now That You Have Her Phone Number

When you finally do call make sure you keep it light and airy, be charming and kinda funny, that'll grab her attention and make her smile saying to herself 'this man is alright!' Keep the conversation short, letting her know that you were just thinking about her and thought you'd call, then say your good-byes, and hang up the phone.

You're now poised to ask her out on that all important first date but don't make that request too soon, give it about a week. Who knows, maybe she's been calling you all the while but if you rush in where Angels fear to tread, you'll just make her feel as if her back is against a wall, she'll think you too hungry and back off.

Remember that thing about not getting a second chance for a first impression? That comes into play once again, the first time was when you met, and you made her smile. Since that first encounter, you should have some kind of an idea what kind of girl she is so dress accordingly. But whatever and however you choose to dress just make sure you're straight on point; shoes clean, shirt and pants pressed.

Don't forget my ShyGuys, you're still fishing, you have her on the hook and now you're trying to reel her in. In addition, just like a fish there'll be moments of resistance. Try not to overdress unless you're going to an event like a fashion show or the like then you come out with both guns blazing; sharper than a needle with a point on both ends! The girl will be proud to be seen with you ...

When it's time to ask for that first date don't go in there all timid. Be strong and confident in the knowledge that her answer will be yes. You're already prepared. You have decided where you want to take her and what it is you two are going to do. Your clothes are laid out, and your hair is freshly cut. Now you're ready for an adventure.

Okay, here we go. Call the girl up and tell her about this event you heard was coming to town or was already there then simply ask 'would you like to go?' Then be quiet and let her answer. Now the date is set and you're happier than a sissy in boy's camp!

Try not to show just how happy you are. Talk to her in the same tone as you would when asking her about the weather, charmingly friendly. The girl can have no idea just how happy you really are because she'll start to think she's all that. The reason she's going is because you came at her strong and assured as if you'd have been surprised if she has said no. Keep her off balance. The thing about a pretty woman is that she's been told she's pretty all of her life so you telling her that same old thing is unoriginal, she's used to it. Moreover, since she is used to being called pretty, she pays particular attention to the men who don't say it. I'm talking about a normal attractive girl and not one of those neurotic ones that need to be told constantly how wonderful they look.

Her little mind is just whirring around trying to figure out why you don't think so, now you've become something different in her life. I'm not saying don't compliment the woman just keep it to something like her clothes, hairdo "I really like those shoes sugar" I might pick out something in her face like dimples or a cute gap in her front teeth and comment on that.

Destiny's child said it right when they said a bug a boo wanted to make them turn their cell phone off, makes them want to break a lease so they can move. Yeah fellas, a bug a boo is someone who bugs women. Someone who calls constantly leaving messages, and she is tired of hearing your voice on the other end of the phone. Leave the girl alone and let her be the bug a boo!

You don't need to know where she is every second of the day, you're gonna have to learn to trust a little bit. If Ms needs some room to breathe needs some 'me' time, let her have it and with your blessings and you go do what it is that you do; catch a movie, or just sit quietly taking a break from all the noise of the world.

When my wife needs some me time, she'll tell me then she'll say "go ahead and say it" "say what honey?" All innocently. "You know you want to say it, then I will say "free at last, free at last, thank God Almighty I'm free at last!" She just starts laughing and goes on her merry way and I enjoy my me time.

You're out there on that first date and you're trying to make a good impression – don't – just be you and enjoy yourself, after all it was you she started liking and not someone else. While you're out there, get her a little something to remember the day by. Oh my, you just happen to be near a flower shop wink- wink;

Go ahead and buy her a white rose, not red. Red means love and white means friendship. Moreover,if you happen to be at the county fair, win or buy her something like a teddy bear, she'll appreciate it. Always keep the mood, atmosphere and conversation light and fun, don't get deep on her. At what point should you approach sex? Don't, never, not ever, not even, nada, no way, don't try it, don't do it, PERIOD!! Now, is there anything about this subject that's unclear? Good… Lets move on.

While talking you're going to have this urge to talk about yourself a lot, try not to do that. Ms Lil Girl wants to get to know you but not all at once. Don't say anything negative and stay away from controversial subjects like politics or religion. Always remember to turn your focus back on her and let her do all of the talking while you do all the listening. If the conversation starts to dry up, pick up something from what she has already said and get her going again. See, that's where listening comes in handy.

We all have our little skeletons in the closet so let yours stay put and watch for what drops out of her mouth. If things look like they're starting to get too deep, change the subject. If she brinks up sex, change the subject. That lets her know that's not all you're interested in. Either she's testing you to see how you handle it or she's gonna have to feel the vibes and make a choice. Now me, I change the subject every time until I'm reasonably sure she's on my team then look out cause here comes Mr. Frank!

Pay attention to red flags. You may wonder what flags to be on the lookout for so here goes; picking her teeth with a fork, no manners, not clean or flatulent. Seriously though, watch out for subtle signs of a possessive nature, the way the corners of her mouth curl up when she sees another woman looking at you or talking to you. Watch closely for any sign of behavior that just gives you the willey's.

One girl stands out in my memory because every time I looked up she was staring at me. At first, I took it for affection, then when it continued, I started to get the shivers, what was she looking at so hard? I know I'm not the most handsome man out there so it couldn't be that, so just what was Ms Creepy sizing me up for? It was a shame that I had to cut her loose because I really liked her, but she would see me talking to other women and just stare at me expressionless. Ooh wee, just got a chill up my spine thinking about her.

Now the date is over, and you've had the time of your life. Everything went perfectly smooth and according to plan, you glance at her, and she smells that rose you gave her and smiling sweetly into the distance. It's time to take her home and you can make small talk about the day, the things you did and saw. You're at her house and she tells you what a wonderful time she had and reaches for the door handle to your car - stop her and tell her you'll come around and get her. You open the door and extend your hand to help her out when she tells you that you're such a gentleman.

Walk her to the door and here comes that awkward moment when you're both standing there looking at each other. Give her a

 Gregory P. Williams

gentle smile and lean in slightly to see if she's waiting for a kiss and if she leans toward you give her that kiss that she's going to judge you by so make it a good one. At this point, she'll either hurry in or invite you in. if she hurries in wish her good night but if she lingers and asks you to come in ... Checkmate.

Here's an afterthought. Make sure you ask for exactly who it is that you want. It's strange but whatever thoughts you put into the ether seems to come true in some form or other. I've learned to think very clearly about who it is I want and in great detail! Call it God, life, universal spirit, whatever you're into; it seems to give you just what you ask for. You say you want a quiet woman, but she doesn't talk at all. You ask for a conversationalist, but she never shuts up. You ask for a sexy and freaky woman, and she is that way with everyone!

They say opposites attract and that may very well be true. My wife and I are so different I sometimes wonder how we stay together. She's a quiet and soft-spoken person whereas I have a forceful and commanding personality. She likes indoor activities like art shows, museums and the like while I like outdoor things like fishing, hiking, biking etc. Nevertheless, with all the differences we seem to complement each other; she has what I lack and I have what she needs Where were we? Oh yeah. You're on your way home and you're grinning like a Cheshire cat.

You're feeling good physically, mentally, and emotionally. This is the place where we shy guys tend to fall in love, and it's way too soon because you'll be in love all by yourself, baby doesn't feel the same way. Now, if you're caught in this trap, you'll find that you're expecting her to act a certain way but she doesn't and why is that you'll ask yourself? Because she doesn't love you! She likes you and at this point that's good enough. She hasn't fallen in love; she's fallen in like.

We've already talked about rushing things, so I won't go into it now. If you've been doing your homework, then you have more than one girl on the line. At this point don't put all your energy into just one, it's like Smoky Robinson said, "you gotta shop around". So, you probably have a date with someone else set for the very near future. Are we having fun yet my fellow ShyGuys?

CHAPTER TWELVE

Once You've Won Them

Okay now, you and Ms Honey Bunny have been going out and everything seems to be going just fine so you can relax now, right? Wrong! You're gonna have to continue to date her if you want to keep things going strong. There's absolutely nothing wrong with taking baby to the movies a couple times or so every month. Dinner out once a week is all good too because it keeps excitement in the game, it just makes her need you more and more. If you're still with the same girl and having a committed relationship, continuing to date her keeps her happy knowing that you still have the hots for her.

Woo hoo! It's time to start meeting each other's family and friends. The two of you have probably met people here and there but now it's time to say, "hello y'all, I'm here to stay". Besides, you need to see where she comes from yanno? Did her uncle Billy seem just a tad crazy? How about mom and her ongoing love affair with Prince Valium? Pops is cool; he just gets his drink on to help him cope. Moreover, didn't he once ask you if you were sure you wanted to be in this family?

By the same token, sweetie gets to meet your uncle Charles, well, at least when he's sober and your brother is your heart and although he is on medication to help keep him centered, you love him, and it hasn't been proven that cousin Jack is smoking crack. Yep, you can both see where the other comes from and now it makes sense that the girl dislikes it when you have a drink but then, now you know why she is on antidepressants.

The unexpected is just that - unexpected -so stay situationally aware that your new lady just might have a psychotic ex-boyfriend and / or girlfriend tucked away somewhere that she's forgotten to tell you about. Then there are other internal things going on like her asking you to help her get her taxes together for the tax man, then drops a box of receipts on your lap.

There are so many things that can come up with Ms She Has a Crazy Uncle so be on notice that you might have to jet at a moment's notice. Now that you know you can better prepare for any eventualities. Take time to really get to know each other. Just how much time you may be asking yourself? - Well, it depends on how well you two are clicking and by that, I mean how close you have become. If you're very close it won't take too long whereas if you're not, it'll take a bit longer. Three or four months should tell you pretty much what you need to know.

We have our ShyGuy faults, defects and shortcomings and she has hers. This is the point that will tell you whether or not the two of you can make it. This is where you find out if you can deal with her inherent craziness and she yours. So, like I've been saying all along -take it slow and easy and you'll be much better off for doing so. Just imagine rushing headfirst into this romance, giving your heart away just to find out too late that the two of you are incompatible. Then you'll have to choose between sticking it out in an unhappy deal or just letting go and walking. Either way it'll hurt your heart so take your time. Now as to who's going to lead this dance. If you let her lead the way, you'll just be miserable.

Someone has to drive the boat so it might as well be you. It's up to you to guide the relationship to where you want to go. I'm going to sound a tad bit sexist here, but we were made to hunt, protect and provide, whereas they were meant to nurture and love. You should be somewhat dominant and she somewhat submissive.

The women reading this are going to get together and roast me over an open pit. Sorry ladies, but I tend to keep it real when I can't keep it right. Men tend to operate from their brain while women are controlled by their emotions. Case in point. Whenever my wife has to handle the bills because I've gone somewhere, the money always comes up short because her belief is; we must pay these bills NOW! She gets scared. When I'm doing it I set a schedule to pay them and they get paid on time according to my time line, thus keeping the maximum amount of money in my accounts at all times. Her heart will flutter, and she'll give it all away.

Your date's best friend's approval -we all know about this one. If her best friend doesn't sign off on you it's going to put a strain on things so when you meet her/him, all that charm you've been working on? It's time to showcase it. You don't have to kiss ass, but you do have to bedazzle that person with your suave and magnetic personality. It's like we already talked about; stand tall and shake hands firmly introducing yourself then pass an offhand compliment in their direction.

See, when they get alone, they're going to compare notes about you so make that first impression a lasting one. If her best friend is female, and she likes what she sees she may throw a flirt your way, just smile and let that fly straight past you. She's probably testing you to see how you respond. Oh yeah, they do that!

"She loves me ... She loves me not ... She loves me-that's right, she don't love you! But why? Cause you're a sucker - but I love her-that's why you're a sucker!" Anyone remember that? I love that line!

I know your heart is all pumped up right now but slow your roll because Ms. Candy Girl isn't there yet. Give her some time and she'll catch up. However, right now she's still feeling you out, lilgirl has probably had her heart tossed about a time or two and now she's cautious. It has nothing to do with you, it's called baggage, and everyone has some. I once dated a girl who would frown every time I took a drink - it seems her previous was a hard drinker with everything that goes along with it. But she told me she didn't have any baggage -so much for that. Just relax and don't be a sucker! I said to be dominant, I didn't mean overbearing -big difference. Don't argue over little things. Sometimes you're going to be right and there'll be times when she is right. Promptly let baby know when you're wrong but just as important or maybe more so, let her know when she is right. Always aim to keep balance in the relationship.

Should big things come up there's no need to argue about that either - discuss it- keep the drama to a minimum. Side note: if she turns out to be a drama queen, kick lil Ms Actress straight to the curb because that's an argument waiting to happen. There'll be times ShyGuys, when you must put your foot down and make your stand known, but you don't have to stomp it like an errant child. When you have ground to stand on, stand tall.

Okay fellas, here I go getting ready to make these women want to hang me from a flagpole. Ladies, we must remake you because you have issues, deep and unresolved I might add. Now we have issues too so don't think I'm picking on you. It's our job to remake you into the women you were meant to be just as it's your job to remake us into the men we're supposed to be. Guys, these women have hidden traits that should be brought out and it's up to you to recognize her inner strengths and beauty and bring them to the forefront, letting here shine like the precious jewel she is. That said, put the chick in check when she needs it, cause if you don't, she'll walk all over your back to the point that you'll think you're in an Oriental massage parlor! If you have special skillz that you haven't told her about now's the time to show off just a little bit.

Let's say you know how to stop a toilet from leaking, and you go to the girl's house and find what? You got it. Fix it. On the other hand, let's say she has so many clothes in her closet that the rod they're hanging from has fallen, ask her if she would like you to put it back up.

 Gregory P. Williams

The average single woman in America has lots of things that you can work on much to her amazement -girl didn't know you had it in you! Same thing for her car or her bike, all you must do is look around and see where you can be handy. Yanno, there's a reason the handyman can come calling on baby when you're at work so make sure the only man she needs is you.

Over the years I've gotten pretty good at fixing things, putting together items she might buy or keeping her computer running smoothly. She says to me all the time "I don't know what I'd do without you" or "I feel sorry for women who don't have a man like you". Make her need you more than she doesn't.

Use special days to your advantage. It's always good to have your lady reference a certain date to some event you planned if nothing more than taking her to the beach on Memorial Day. She'll remember that beautiful Labor Day weekend when you took her to the theme park or Christmas at home in front of the fireplace. You're building memories for her that'll last a lifetime.

Chapter Thirteen

The Same Thing It Took to Get Her, It's Gonna Take the Same Thing to Keep Her

Don't think that because you have her you can stop doing the things you've been doing, that's one of the biggest mistakes we men tend to make. We think that we can stop being charming. Give her that very special wink that she's come to know. By contrast, she still needs to wake up her to the smell of fresh coffee being brewed and breakfast being made.

Now is not the time to stop going for rides out to the country for absolutely no reason other than you want to spend time together. Yeah fellas, you're still extending your hand to help her out of the car and opening doors for her or lighting her cigarette if she smokes. Continue to give her that sexy sly smile when driving down the Street and placing your hand on her oh so smooth thigh!

The woman has gotten used to you bringing her presents so don't stop. I'll say it again -the same thing it took to get your baby, it's gonna take the same thing to keep her. It shouldn't be too hard to do since you've already grown accustomed to bringing her candy because she has had a hard day at work.

It doesn't take a whole lot of money to keep the girl happy. Once when I had very little money, I found a piece of wood and carved it into a heart. I sanded and polished it then found a silver chain to hang it from and gave it to her. The girl was so happy that she cried because I thought so much of her to take the time to do that.

Regarding sex, I'd say that if you started by sexing her often, you'll have to continue doing that or she will think you're tired of her. I don't have a whole lot to say about the sex thing other than the woman's got to have it more than occasionally. And don't be a 'Captain Quick Draw' and get yours before she gets hers. Learn to slow roll it with passion. Women don't particularly care for a man who's too fast, and always let her know through words and actions that you still appreciate her.

I could write an entire book on conversation and how to keep it going strong or on honest and open communication and just how important that is to a healthy and happy relationship. Remember how when you first met her you had a thousand things to talk about? Well ShyGuys, you'll have to keep those lines of communication open and the conversation fresh and new. The way I keep my conversation fresh is by talking to other women and men. From the men I get to hear what's working and what's not working for them and with the women I can try out new and exciting topics and see how they respond while listening to what they have to say. I'll take all of that back home and use it on babygirl, that way my conversation doesn't get stale and I always have something new to say. Now fellas, I didn't say go out there and screw everything in sight, but friendly flirtation is okay.

Some men think they can forget about being on their best behavior. They think it's okay to sit around in their boxers all day picking their noses and scratching their back sides -that's just wrong on a whole lot of levels. You got the girl by being dressed all the time with a clean car and now your car is sitting outside needing a bath. There's nothing wrong with watching Sunday's game but at least wear pajama bottoms and resist the urge to be flatulent in her presence cause that's not cute at all. There used to be a time when you'd sip your soup with a spoon and now, you're eating cornflakes out of a skillet. Always maintain that persona that swept her off her feet.

We ShyGuys have a tendency not to be assertive. Good guys really do finish last and aren't we the good guys here? In order not to finish last we must set priorities and rules and stand firm by them. Women absolutely do not respect weakness in a man. I know just how you feel about wanting to let her have her way because it makes her happy, but in the end, it'll make us very unhappy plus she'll start to take you for granted. Whether we're in this for the long haul or just for some short-term fun we have to maintain control. It's so easy to cave in to her demands especially right after she's ridden our bodies like a freight train running down the track, so we have to remain strong.

Most girls like you to show them affection in public and there's nothing wrong with that. Don't you like to have her show you affection? We older ShyGuys don't really have a problem with that, it's the younger ones who for some reason are worried about what their friends would say. It seems like such a little thing, but many females hold this in high priority, I guess it's their way of marking their territory. At any rate, it wouldn't hurt to put your arm around her waist then pull her close.

It has been several months, and her parents just love the way you treat lil mama. The girl is happy, so the parents are happy too, at least half of the parents are. If dad is anything like I was back then, he's not going to like you no matter how hard you try. Why is that? There's something about the thought of a man intimately touching our little girl; it just makes us want to choke them until puke comes out of their ears. Sorry about that ... had a flashback.

Now where was I? Anyway, I was dating this one girl whose parents were rich and it seemed that dad hadn't liked any of her previous boyfriends. Well, I was determined not to kiss his rich behind and told him the only thing I wanted from him was his daughter. Well, she came to me one day and told me that her daddy

     Gregory P. Williams

respected me. I smiled and stuck out my chest "so he likes me huh?" She said "no, I didn't say all that" so fellas, work on mom!

It's been a lot of fun so far, Ms Ooh Wee is falling head over heels in love with you and all is well in the world. At this point I hope you've decided what it is you want to do with her because she is probably thing about your future together and a wedding dress. So far, you've done everything right and you may have found Ms Right for You, who knows, maybe you're even thinking about kids running around the house. What is there to do next, you may ask? Well, keep doing what you've been doing to make the two of you happy. Take a breather and enjoy the moment.

CHAPTER FOURTEEN

The Best Places to Find Women

Women can be found everywhere excluding men's prisons (well, I guess you find them there too) and that sort of thing. Cruises are in my opinion the absolute best place to find incredible numbers of willing and searching women. The women on board are looking to be laid. Theme cruises are nice because you have many like-minded people together. There are more theme cruises than I can count: jazz, single, young people, gay, straight, undecided you name it. The thing about this is that you can let your hair down and be and do whatever you want; what happens onboard stays on board.

Special events are still a good place to go because there you can get to see the beauties that you normally don't get the chance to see. These are the ones who usually go out only during those times. If you're in a church, then you already know what I'm about to say. There are many women there just waiting for someone they can call husband.

The number two lake to go fishing is the Internet! There are so many dating sites out there it's just a wonder one doesn't get lost. There are sites for immediate sex and for long term relationships, there are those that cater to BDSM and that would be bondage, degradation, sadism and masochism. You have vampires with their attendant donors along with dominant/submissive role play. Anything and everything you can think of is somewhere on the net. However, you must be careful here because people can, do and will be anything and anyone they want to be while hiding behind the keyboard. One of the saddest moments is when you're all geared up to finally meet Ms. Beautiful in person then come to find out that the picture she gave you was not hers at all. This one girl told me that she had dated this guy online for several months and he seemed to be just what she was looking for, six foot two inches tall and one hundred-eighty pounds, coconut brown skin and bald head with two gold hoops hanging out of one ear. When she finally did meet him, he was five foot three, one hundred-thirty pounds, white with Sandy blond hair. She asked him why he lied and he said he wanted her to like him for him ... Well doggone it, five foot three does not round up to six feet two, potnah! I learned, after two or three of those faux pas that I had to get a web cam (tellin' my age again) and I highly recommend you do the same so you can see who you're talking to but you have to be careful here too because Ms Movie Star will have her friend get on cam for her.

Remember what I said about not getting a second chance to make a first impression? Well, I was about to meet the girl and I was ready; Stetson hat Freshly brushed, snakeskin boots shining. I mean I had a leather duster draped to my ankles, and wearing a real tough suit with all the bling at my command because I figured her to be one of those women who bit at that kinda thing. I pulled up and knocked on the door, asked for her and the woman at the door said, "I'm her". She looked nothing like her picture. I was so disappointed. Needless to say, that particular thing didn't work out because if she lies about who she is, she'll lie about everything else.

The S.A.M. approach is by far the most effective approach. It's been working for you so don't stop; it's as they say, 'don't fix it, if it ain't broke!' Have you noticed and doesn't it tickle you the way they look at you when you say the strangest things?

The Say Anything Method works with most women and in most situations. 'Did you just hear her thinking that she wanted to go to dinner?' (Tell her that). You always get some kind of response, be it good and she says yes, or bad where she just looks at you. It doesn't matter. What does matter is that you got a response, so tell her to get out of line and call 'next' if she gives you a less than positive answer

The only way to get good at anything is to practice. The same holds true for attracting women so practice every chance you get. Now what I would do for practice exercise was to see just how many girls I could walk up to each day. Give yourself a quota and say to yourself 'I need to talk to ten women today and get ten phone numbers. What would usually happen to me is that I would talk to those ten and maybe get eight phone numbers, eighty percent, not too shabby! I would then go home and think about what I had said, did or how I blundered with the couple of girls that I'd missed. My ultimate goal was to get very good and be very comfortable around women. Practice fellas, all the time from the moment you get up to the time you go to bed.

Keeping track of all the girls you've run across helps to keep mistakes down to a minimum, tracking all the errors along the way. Yes ShyGuys, keeping an eye on when and where can reap big rewards. Tracking the different places you go also helps to see a pattern of just who you've met and where, then you say to yourself, 'The Internet is good, but the cruise was better'. Using the analogy of fishing again, you see that this lake has the most bass while this other lake has the biggest. That river over there has golden trout in it, but the lake you visited last week had huge crappie! You have to remember that the different types of women are going to be found at various places like say for instance, the gold digger is going to be found at an upscale and Swank lounge for the most part but the hoochie Mama is likely to visit the local watering hole. Look over there! See the good girl coming out of the church door? or the Twerkaholic strutting her stuff at the mall and the hood rat walking into the corner store? Yes ShyGuys, keeping an eye on when and where reaps big benefits!

Dating several women at one time can sometimes be extremely stressful so always be careful here and tell the truth so you don't get

 Gregory P. Williams

caught up in a lie. Side note: the best lie is 99.9% true and remember to answer the question she's asking like 'do you have the time?' And you answer, 'it's three honey'. That is not what she asked you. She asked do you have the time to which the answer would be 'yes'. If you can't repeat the question word for word, then you don't understand the question. Okay I confess, I once wanted to be a lawyer! My memory isn't all that great so I have to tell the truth because I will forget what lie I told!

Back to the topic at hand. Dating several women gives you not only flexibility but also gives you choices. Like I said, we ShyGuys tend to get hung up on just one and when that doesn't pan out, we're heartbroken. Having several means you're not dependent on any particular one. Besides, when one starts playing those sweet little games they like to play, you can cut them loose without it bothering you overmuch. Sometimes the hardest thing to do is cut someone loose. But then, for your sanity and peace of mind you must shake them off periodically. Now you have to decide just which way to do that causing as little turmoil and drama as possible.

With all this new technology and social behavior, some people find it easiest and appropriate to simply text her with the news; if you do so by Twitter you have about 140 characters to say what your heart and mind feels. Next at bat is the 'letter' which is similar to the text except that it's more personal because it's usually handwritten, and you can say more. The phone call is better in a lot of cases because you can hear the tone of her voice and what she's trying so desperately to convey. My personal and number one choice is in person. That way I can gaze deeply and thoughtfully into her *lying eyes*, and she can look into mine and see the sincerity with which I'm throwing her under the bus.

At some point, ol' girl is going to want to feel as if she is number one in your book so it's time to 'stake your claim'. Personally, I'd let her know that she is number one but that there is a number two, number three etc. -Hey ladies, I'm just keeping it real -I'd be more prone to doing that (staking my claim) quietly, with Babygirl oblivious to what

I'm doing. I would merely display it and not just say it. When you don't drive her around town, she'll think you're keeping her a secret and not wanting others to see you with her.

By this time, you should be pretty much comfortable with walking up to strange, exotic, and beautiful women. Remember my fellow ShyGuys, she has dreams just like you. She has hopes for that very special someone just like you. In other words, she is almost just like you except that she squats when she takes a leak and you stand, so don't put her up in some kind of shrine because she's just a girl - nothing more, nothing less.

I've spoken to a lot of people, men in particular who tell me that it's hard to just walk up to someone of the opposite sex and pull a conversation out of thin air. I say to them "act like that person is the same sex as you" and that should settle your nerves if you're still having those types of problems. I've already admonished you about putting her up on a pedestal because she will sprinkle when she tinkles right down in your face, but like I say, maybe you're into warm spring rains.

Getting back to leaving home with your best face on basics. Since we don't know when or where Ms Dream Girl is going to show up, we need to make sure we're showered, dressed nicely, and smelling good because she could be walking through the in door while you're about to walk out. Your shoes need to be clean along with your ride as these are the two things she'll notice first. A dirty car and shoes say a whole lot about you.

Now I know you're not going to be neat all the time so just try to make it most of the time. The other day I was out and had gotten my ride cleaned, vacuumed, and glowing like new money. Well, the following day while out, it rained and let me tell you it must've been raining mud because my truck was caked with it. So here I am going to the store on my way home and who should show up? That's right, Ms Yeah Baby! She took one look at my vehicle, one look at me-I'd left home in my 'at home relaxing clothes' and turned her head away.

 Gregory P. Williams

See, opportunity happens just that quick and when you least expect it so stay ready!

I guess by now you've heard it said about the lottery that you can't win if you don't play. The same thing holds true here. If you don't get out there and play, the odds of you winning are very slim to none. I tell people this and they reply with "well, don't you lose money at the lottery a lot?" I say "yes, that's true but the odds of my winning increase with each time I play". (gotta check the lottery stats on that one) but you see what I'm saying.

I have a good friend who stays home most of time. He's got the bling, the car, the conversation and all of the trappings that would make a woman take a bite at him, but he doesn't get out there and then wonders why the girls aren't around. Moreover, that holds true for we ShyGuys; we don't spend a whole lot of time around the ladies then wonder where they're all at. So, get out there because there are a bunch of women looking for you but can't find you because you're not out there on the track. It's a craps shoot and that's all fine and dandy. Sometimes you win, sometimes you lose and sometimes the game gets called on account of weather, but you have to roll the dice to win. All of this may seem like a lot of work, but it really isn't. What we're doing here is changing ourselves, the way we look and the way we act, how we now respond to the world around us. Every day and in every way, we must hone our skillz to the point that we are now razor sharp. The big payoff comes when we're surrounded by pretty girls coming and going in and out of our lives. And the new found self-esteem and confidence that comes with knowing that whatever we want out there we can now go get.

CHAPTER FIFTEEN

We All Want a Pretty Girl

The pretty scale is that mental measuring stick we have for the ladies with zero being so un-pretty that we chew off our own arm the following morning just so we don't wake her up and we can leave her place quietly. Any girl that approaches zero is so coyote ugly that we can't walk down the street with her and still hold our head up. By contrast, on the other end of the scale a ten means she is so pretty that if she were to pee down our backs, we'd swear it was lemonade on a summers day! I mean she is so fine that heaven hired detectives to find and bring her back. This is the girl we've been looking for our entire lives.

You'll probably think I'm smoking some real good herbal, when I say this but ... Pretty girls are just about the easiest to get. Really. The reason is that they are pretty. Other men are afraid to approach her for fear of rejection. However, the truth is this; she's probably lonelier than you are! That's right, little Ms Lonely is probably waiting for someone to just say hello to her. Can you imagine going through life thinking no one wants to talk to you and equally afraid to speak to someone of a different sex? So, it really is amazing that we ShyGuys don't have more of them. I learned a long time ago to just walk up and say hi. You'll be surprised at the response you get. And if she is one of those pretty girls that thinks the world owes her a favor, and for those, you move on cause you don't want that type anyway, "sorry honey, next!"

The subject of looks can sometimes be tricky. We all want a gorgeous girl but at the same time we do not want to eliminate a possible match. Therefore, the question is this: just how important are looks to you. For some, good looks are synonymous with character, which couldn't be further from the truth. To some, a pretty face is of paramount importance. For me on the other hand, if a woman is just attractive enough for me to be able to walk down the street with her and still be able to make eye contact with another man passing by, I'm okay. Maybe I'm being just a tad bit shallow but, I don't want to date a She-wolf just as you ladies don't want to date a grizzly bear (although some of you do like it rough) we will get to the subject of the not so pretty girl in just a bit.

Outward appearances are okay but Ms Way Too Fine needs to have an inward beauty as well. Here's some more of my math: pretty face+ lousy personality= not worth it! It truly is a shame when you walk up to that curvaceous and lovely creature only to have her frown in the worse way making her completely unattractive. Girls like that are useless in my book. They're nothing more than eye candy because they are unfit to do anything else. These girls believe that they only have to use their looks to get what they want. Never realizing that good looks don't last, but a good personality does. When we first notice their behavior, we must kick them to the curb with all of the gusto we can muster, so in a nutshell, beauty shouldn't be the first thing you want in a girl although it is the first thing that we see.

Other men are going to look. Having issues about that right now? Jealousy is something we cannot afford. Remember, women are like buses; one comes along every twenty minutes so we have no need to be jealous, we can always catch another. Yanno, the time to start sweating matters is when the men stop looking. That is an indication that your girl is either unattractive, never was attractive, or isn't attractive anymore so take it as high praise when they stare and try to steal her from you. If you've applied yourself correctly the odds of someone taking a girl from you are mighty slim. The other guys are probably using those tired old lines she's used to hearing or the ones you told her to watch out for. So, when they flirt with her just smile confidently and go on about your business.

Most pretty women know they're pretty and that can be a problem. First of all, when speaking to a pretty woman never tell her she's attractive because she's used to being called that all her life. In addition, we're being someone who does different things so say different things. The ones who don't know they're attractive are some of the sweetest girls you're likely to run across and don't know why guys don't approach them. Moreover, if she knows that she is good-looking then here comes Ms Hell on a Westerly Breeze cause little girl surely does think she's all that. So, you must put her in check from the very beginning by letting her know through your actions that you don't think she is that red velvet cake with chocolate frosting. Remember, the first thing you want to do is also the last thing that you want to do; don't tell her she's pretty.

Woo hoo, here comes that wallet breaker Ms High Maintenance herself and the girl needs to have that $2,000 weave re-done. And don't you just love the way she runs her fingers through your hair and play with the hair on your chest with those expensive fingernails? Yes ShyGuys, that oh so attractive lady needs all kinds of things so she will be beautiful for you (at least that's what she says).

Then there are those times when she spends the entire day at the spa with the girls getting facials, manicures, and pedicures. Her 'me' time has your bank account screaming for mercy 'hep me, hep me!' The cold part about it all is that she almost has you believing that it's your idea to keep her looks up. Now I say to them "what were you doing about that before I came along?" Cause Ms Shorty Pie looked like she had all that handled when you met her.

Here come the ones who are so hopelessly and helplessly used to being admired. They strut and preen like that 'ol pheasant up in that tree. Those types are really easy to catch seeing as all you have to do is be where they can see you and watch you being charming with all the ladies all the while purposefully ignoring her. She is wondering

     Gregory P. Williams

why you're the only one not noticing how cute she is. Eventually she will find a reason to get next to you like, "may I borrow your pen?" Or "it sure is hot in here" or some other pretext to speak to you. Listen ShyGuys, when you catch her sneaking a peek at you from across the room that means she is saying 'yes' to herself then when she steps up to you, she's saying 'let's go have some fun' and all you have to do is not screw it up! she wants you to say something clever to her although she doesn't know it. You know ShyGuys, once I found out just how easy these girls were, I wondered why I was so afraid of them and nervous about them in the first place. They are so predictable you can almost set your watch by them.

You know those pretty eyes she had? well she pulled out her contacts and threw them on the couch, and that pretty hair ... She pulled off her wig and threw it on the couch ... She had the prettiest smile. she pulled out her dentures and threw them on the couch ... Baby had the cutest shape ... She pulled off that girdle and threw it on the couch and those shapely legs? Surgical pantyhose ... Took 'em off and threw them on the couch, then she pulled off that sexy dress and threw it on the couch, then she jumped in the bed ... hell, I jumped on the couch!

Am I the only one that has had that kind of experience? Write me and let and let me know, I would love to hear your story! Yep fellas, we should all get together and sue those cosmetic manufacturers for having us wake up after a night of fun only to have that lovely creature last night turn into skeletor in the morning.

A good looking 'good girl' does not look as good as a good looking 'skank'. I guess that's because the skank has some serious curb appeal going on whereas the good girl is just ... There. I suppose by now you can tell that I have a penchant for the more outgoing woman. And it's true because doggone it, the girls in the city 'sho look pretty. And the way they walk, oh my! I'm throwing in this little side note because some of you may be thinking 'good girl, good girl, I want one'. The good girl is not a lot of fun just so you know, although she is unmatched in the loyalty and caring department.

Sometimes you have to let them know that they can be replaced, maybe not easily or happily, but replaced. If Ms Stuck Up is still sticking her nose up, then tell her to check herself before she wrecks herself! Why would you want to replace that raving beauty you ask? Well, females like that tend to get tiresome after a while.

I've known fellas who've gotten together with that almost useless pretty girl and more than half of them regret that they did. I mean come on sweetie, let me use the mirror for a bit. Have you ever noticed that when a good-looking woman has a pitifully lousy attitude that it takes away from her beauty? Similarly, an average looking girl with a fantastic personality appears to be much prettier.

Usually, this female will settle down when and if you take the time to let her know that she is not all that. In fact, she should be happy that you took the time to speak to her in the first place and taking it further still, let me take my hello back! Oh, and by the way, while I'm at it let me kick your cute behind straight down the way!

During challenging economic times when money is tight, then a twenty-dollar weave may be the appropriate thing to do. However, when times are good and the money is flowing and she still has a twenty dollar weave you need to look at her again, cause ... Dayuum ... Somethin' wrong. Looks like I have to add an addendum here. I was just told by a woman that there is no such thing as a twenty-dollar weave. I must disagree because just like Bigfoot, I've seen them running around! And Dayuum, ain't it skurry!!

   Gregory P. Williams

CHAPTER SIXTEEN

A Moment for the Not So Pretty Girl

My grandmother, who we called mama, used to tell me to marry an ugly girl who can cook because you only have to get used to her once. Now a Pretty girl you have to get used to her twice, because first you have to get used to that oh so attractive new person in your life, then when she gets old and ugly you have to get used to her again! I briefly dated a girl who used to say that I thought she was ugly because I made her wear my motorcycle helmet. I said, "no honey, I just want to keep you safe" or she would say, "you only come to see me at night, you must think I'm ugly" and I would reply, "no honey, I just like the way the stars sparkle in your eyes!" Ya gotta be quick fellas!

She may not have been the cutest thing around, but she was sure sweet .... I wonder whatever happened to her. Anyway, the point is that although she is not what and who you want, she may still be that girl. Yanno, the unattractive girl can sometimes be a diamond in the rough; a rare jewel that only needs to be polished with love and affection. Here is someone with an unassuming nature, kind and gentle. But let us be honest here, there are some not so pretty girls who are angry at the world for coming out that way. They are noisy and abusive - mean spirited and think that because you smile at them, you must think they're all that or they tend to resent a handsome man looking their way for settling for them. Her marketable value is based solely on her looks ... 'po thang.

The not so pretty girl is not unattractive through and through, she does have other beautiful qualities if you just look for them, at least most of the time. Okay, so her feet look like she should be perched up in that tree! So what? She may have the most beautiful breasts you have ever seen, or her smile just radiates loveliness and charm. It doesn't really matter then that she is also a little overweight, there's just more for you to love.

Besides, the girl can always go get a pedicure or see the doctor about problematic feet. I once dated this girl for about three days and couldn't go on any longer because her big toes were at right angles to her feet. They were bent sideways pointing at her baby toes. One night she came home from work and pulled her shoes off and said "Honey, rub my feet for me" I took one look at those hooves and fled. Had I found something stunning in her I might have stayed but as it was I did not.

The unattractive girl is usually quite bright seeing as she was not doing a lot of dating in school, so she spent her time studying. She definitely is not the dumb blond type oh no. You can converse with her on any number of levels. Most of the time you can find her sitting somewhere reading a book. Hey, why not go on over there and say hi, you'll probably be rewarded with the most radiant smile you have ever seen. You will usually find her in the company of good-looking girls knowing they are 'draw cards' and maybe she just might catch one of the fellas her posse didn't want. This girl is just as sweet as pecan pie. Speaking of which, the girl can cook her butt off. It's just like Mama used to say "marry an ugly girl that can cook" she is oh so very easy to love with her easy-going nature and style. ShyGuys, just because you now know how to get the pretty one, let us not forget about the not so pretty girl.

A pretty girl has nowhere to go but down as time marches on, but the not so pretty girl can only go up! That's right fellas, Ms Lady

     Gregory P. Williams

is sporting that $1500 weave made of human hair imported from Brazil and the like. She is wearing the same high heels as that cute gold digger, and doesn't she look good! Yep, that unassuming lady has style and finesse, guys honk their horns for her until she turns around and they say 'oh damn' but keep on looking nonetheless because her inner beauty has her face glowing softly as if moonlight had somehow come down and surrounded her face.

She picks clothes that accentuate her personality and don't those clothes look good on her. Ms Baby Doll was blessed with a figure so nice that a blind man could see her! Some of you might want to cut that chicken off at the neck but that body is jammin'! The way that not so good-looking girl walks makes up for her looks and when other men see you with her, they know the reason why. Although Ms Sweetie is a butter face (everything looks good on her but her face) she still commands attention. I know this girl who has a walk that will make a man change religions! Nevertheless, she is a butter face and that's fine because she has a sexy, almost raspy voice that will make you think all sorts of thoughts.

She must live at Tiffany's because just like the gold digger this lady is blinging too. She knows she's not particularly attractive, so she surrounds herself with flypaper; those trappings that'll catch a man. You could almost say that she puts on a pre-thought-out costume when she goes out. There she goes just around the corner, and she has more glitter than a spinner bait! Yes gentlemen, she uses every trick at her command to entice men to come to her. Her makeup is put on flawlessly and her eyes have this mischievous look in them because she knows someone is going take her home.

The really scary part is when you wake up the next morning after kissing and licking all that expensive makeup off her face and you can now see what she really looks like and like I said earlier, makes you want to chew your arm off. Nevertheless, you have to admit that it was fun; that girl knows what she's doing and that's how you end up walking down the street with her with your head hung down thinking 'just how did this happen?'

Unlike the gold digger, this lady seldom has her hand out because she knows that would be pushing things a bit. Therefore, she has learned to be independent since she thinks she can't depend on a man to take care of her. Side note: an unattractive girl is harder to catch because she thinks that you think that because she is ugly, she must be desperate and subsequently easy to get so she does everything to prove you wrong. The not so pretty girl usually isn't flighty, she is normally pretty steady, and she spoils herself outrageously since because it's harder for her to get a handsome man, she may as well buy herself things.

We haven't covered the matter of children in detail yet so let us do that now. Ahh, children ... those precious cherubs running and playing ... Laughter dancing in the air like celestial wind chimes ...

Okay whatever. Those little crumb snatchers are cute as can be but often times get in your way. The mother doesn't know how to keep them in check, and she won't let you. So here you are trying to have a quiet and romantic conversation while those devil spawned, demon seeds are crawling all over your lap and pouring red Kool-Aid on your brand new $600 gray Stetson hat! Oh no he didn't! did that little ... Just smear chocolate icing on your pant leg? C'mere ya little ... If you were thinking that you and Lil Mama were gonna be knockin boots this afternoon you have another thought coming. And don't let that child be in his teens because he has a big problem with you screwing his mother! Did I say child? No. He's an adult now and he knows exactly what you're doing to his mother behind that closed door. Oh, and do not leave your wallet laying around, you may find that it is a shade lighter than when you laid it down. Yes fellas, like my old man used to say, follow an ugly woman home and something ugly'll open the door!

Compared to the pretty girl, the not so pretty girl can often times come out in the lead because she knows that she has to be good in other areas in order to make up for looks. By contrast, the pretty girl is usually just that ... Pretty. Since men are falling over themselves trying to get to her, she never had to learn other skills in order to get

     Gregory P. Williams

and keep a man. Ms Unattractive may not be the prettiest girl in a room but quite probably she could end up being the best. Just because you caught that fish in muddy water doesn't mean it won't taste good!

CHAPTER SEVENTEEN

What Women Say They Want vs. What They Really Want

Women are always talking about how they want a challenge in a man. A challenge is something competitive where someone wins and someone loses like in basketball then, when she loses, we are back to being called dogs again. Now if you explain to her just what a challenge is and what she is asking for she will tell you "No, that's not what I want" she then changes her verbiage and says, "I want someone who can stimulate my mind". As far as I know, stimulation can mean many things like; incite as in 'let's incite a riot' or fire up as in 'she was sure fired up at him for winking at another woman, then there's motivate as in 'feed her lots of BS and motivate her to do what we want'. In addition, if she actually catches you with said woman her mind will be seriously stimulated! So, whether it be challenging or stimulating, Ms Dizzy in the Head is looking for the wrong thing. For some strange reason she wants a relationship to be difficult. Go figure.

Another item on the list is about having a job. There are three types of men out here:

1.   Working for someone
2.   Has someone working for them
3.   Out of work

Numbers one and two are pretty much obvious, but number three hmm ... Here we have this fella, everything is right about him, but she doesn't want him because he doesn't have a job at the moment. So instead of picking the right guy with no job (only hopes and ambitions) she will run straight to the wrong guy because of his outward appearance.

Yanno, years ago I found myself out of work for a long period of time, but I was filling out applications all day everyday trying to catch a break. Well, early one evening I walked to a local lounge (walked because I didn't have the money to fix my car) went inside and who do you think I saw? Ms Might Be Wonderful sitting alone at the bar. Well, I walked over to the bar and spoke "how are you?" She replied after looking me up and down, "obviously better than you" then turned away. Let me tell you I was hurt. I knew my clothes weren't in the best shape, but they were washed and ironed. I'd worn down the heels on those used to be expensive shoes, but they were polished. I held my head up and sipped my drink then walked home. A year later I'm at this very chic and swank nightclub with the woman who ended up being my wife.

By then I had recovered from my previous financial situation and was wearing an expensive and nice fitting suit. I had on black snakeskin cowboy boots (I guess you can tell I like snakeskin boots!) Black leather coat that hung down to my ankles with a dark gray Stetson hat sitting on my head. I had bling on my hands and dangling from my left ear. Oh yeah, the girls were eyeballing me something fierce! Well, I looked up and who should I see? Yep, sitting at the bar was that same woman wearing the very same olive-green dress with epaulets on the shoulders she was wearing the last time I saw her. I looked at my yet to be wife "honey? Do you remember the story about the woman in the green dress? Well, there she is I'll be right back". She replied, "you're a bigger and better man than that ... Let it go" I smiled wickedly "no I'm not. I won't feel right about myself if I don't clown her just a little bit" I stood up and walked over to the bar.

Standing next to her, I was chatting with the bartender in my naturally deep voice (I made it real mellow just for her) while feeling her eyes crawl all over me. I turned and said, "You don't remember me, do you?" She said, "I could never forget someone like you". So I took her on a trip back down memory lane until her eyes lit up with recognition. I said "see that woman sitting over there wearing that fur coat? That could've been you, never judge a book by its cover" and I casually strolled back to my table leaving her with her mouth wide open and her jaw hanging down to her chest!

With the information you've gotten here you don't necessarily need a car but, for your numbers to increase dramatically you want one. Since time immemorial, a different sex has always focused on the man and his ride. First it was that nice horse compared to that nag the other fella had. And then there was that very pretty horse drawn carriage. Now it's that automobile with that fresh from the detailer shine.

We ShyGuys must use all of the bait at our command and available to us. It doesn't have to be fancy, just something that is clean and well-maintained. It's as I said earlier, some girls wouldn't know an expensive car if it jumped up and ran them over! Have no doubt, Ms Young Thang is very interested in your having a car. Besides, you can't pull up to that ritzy restaurant and have the valet park your bike!

Gone are the days when you could comfortably and happily live in mom's basement, putting your dirty clothes in a hamper for her to wash and fold. For some strange and arcane reason your current fling seems to think there's something terribly wrong with that. They don't completely understand the man/child phenomenon; the biggest difference between men and boys are the price of their toys! Well

     Gregory P. Williams

fellas, now we're being forced to grow up, at least somewhat. The lady wants to have her privacy when she comes to visit us and that's understandable. Let's get out there fellas and get our own place. For the older ShyGuys, we already have our own ... Everything, so we don't have this particular worry.

One day my older brother and I were standing in mom's front yard talking. Not long after, our mother and two younger sisters joined us. One of the girls asked us about our opinion on some matter or other, when brother and I turned toward mom. The older of the sisters said, "why are you looking at mother?" And we replied in unison "we're waiting for our opinion" she said, "you two are such mama's boys" and once again in unison we replied "and your point being?" Just thought I would throw that story in there.

Have any of you ever walked up to a woman and said "all I know about you is your physical aspect and I like what I see, let's go have sex and get to know one another" by the way, say that or something like that to enough women and one will eventually say okay!

Most women will say something negative but it all boils down to "I don't want you to want me for sex, I want you to make love to my mind" or some variation of that theme. So, she wants to be mind fu*ked, okfine. Then, when we do as she asks, we're back to being dogs again. I tell ya, a Man can't win for losing.

So, if she does not want us to lust after her, just what is it then that she does want? Once you have screwed her mind like she wants and then do not screw her physically she has a problem! "Why don't you make love to me?" Cause you didn't want me to! Apparently, she does not have a clue as to what she wants. Now me, I want my girl to lust after me real hard.

They say they want an honest man but that really is not true. You don't believe me you say? Then tell her what you really want from her and just how quickly you want it then watch her, as she doesn't respect your truthfulness. Let's say you go out and get a little more than tipsy and end up in another woman's bed, tell your girl that and see if she wants honesty. See fellas, she only wants the truth when it does not have to do with anything of consequence. When she asks if those jeans make her behind look big tell her "No honey, your behind makes those jeans look small!" And see what happens.

So now, if she really and truly does not want an honest man, what's left that she does want? Yep, you got it, a liar. But because we ShyGuys want to keep lying to a bare minimum we must continue our search for someone who truly wants the honest man and once we find that rare woman, we must hold on to her. 'I want you to love me, only me, and no one else but me!" That's what she thinks and that's what she says but we all know that there are different kinds of love. Like love for your mom or your siblings, love for your best friend who happens to be an attractive girl. Ahh man! Did I just say girlfriend? ooh wee, let the drama begin!!

I don't know about you, but my personal opinion is that a fella who only hangs around with other fellas is suspect of being just a little bit gay, that's right I said it; gay, more gay, gayer still! Now I fancy myself somewhat of a poet, can you imagine me getting up during the halftime festivities and start reciting poetry to a room full of guys who've just finished watching and cheering on big sweaty men touching each other's asses on the playing field? It just doesn't work. Now give me a room full of women who just finished watching a girly flick, now that's appreciation!

It appears that I have to add an addendum here. My wife just read some of this and informed me that I was alienating women with children, guys who huddle together to watch and or play sports and gay people. So just for the record let me say that I love kids; there's nothing like a house full of the little rug rats to make a house feel like a home. And guys who huddle together? Do your thang, I ain't mad at 'cha. And insofar as gays go? I really don't care who's screwing who. Okay? Everybody happy now? Sheesh! So touchy ...

They say that they want gifts for no other reason than you happen to have some cash in your pocket. Now ladies, we want gifts for no

 Gregory P. Williams

reason too so don't think you have a monopoly on wanting. I used to buy presents just because, then two things happened in my life; I had bought a diamond, ruby and emerald ring for someone I ended up marrying (the first time). She told me it was too expensive and to take it back, which of course I did, and never bought her anything else. Then there was another girl I wanted to marry and so I bought her an ivory comb and brush set and got the same response. Needless to say, I don't buy presents just because anymore. Well, not often.

She won't say that she wants the one the other girls want but that's just what's going on. For some strange reason, Ms Gotta Have That Man craves what she thinks she can't have and isn't the guy the other women want the one she thinks she can't live without? This guy has been used like an old dish rag by all those women and the new girl doesn't understand that grass don't grow on a well-used playground. (An old pimp said that). Besides, the men who have girls chasing them all the time don't really have anything to say because they've never had to learn that. She does not know and will not find out until she has been with him for a while that he doesn't even speak all that well. I know this woman who went after the pretty boy and married him only to find out later that he was pretty much illiterate.

Here we go again ladies. You place so much emphasis on a man looking good that you can't see past the exterior. Listen, let me say this again. A good-looking man is just like a good-looking woman in that he's been getting by on this looks and so has never learned any other life skills. Women have been throwing themselves at him his entire life, so he never developed a conversational style of his own. Therefore, while you're out there searching take note of the not so good-looking guy and you may find that you've found someone worth holding onto. The not so good-looking man has learned not only how to get the girl but how to keep her as well. When you have such high standards, you set yourself up for failure every time.

I must have an old-fashioned and out of date idea of what romance is because whenever I lavish my affections and attention on a woman, she runs the other way and then when I start ignoring her, she runs back to me. What's up with that? So fellas, when she says that she wants romance I think it is more like she needs someone she thinks she can keep a finger on. I used to know a girl who almost had a breakdown because she did not have someone to worship her every move.

Now ladies let's be reasonable. The only man who does not look at other gorgeous women with at least some lust is gay, the next man who does not look is too gay, the man after that is gayest of all! Now that you know this check to see if your man looks or not because if he doesn't look, he's suspect. And no, I am not homophobic at all it's just that some things add up and some things add up to being suspect, yanno? On the down low as they say.

These sociopathic and neurotic women swear they want a good man, but it seems to me that they really don't. The qualities and characteristics of a good man are the exact opposite of what they call strong men. Let's see here-a good man is honest, and we've already talked about how honest you can't be. Then there is tender, show a woman your tender side and she will think you weak. Show her your romantic side and she thinks she can walk all over you. So, we must maintain that aloof attitude if you wish to keep Ms She doesn't Know What She Wants in line.

Tell me my fellow ShyGuys, what is it with women and time? For some archaic reason that completely eludes me, it is we who must always be on time. On the other hand, they can be as late as they want to and call it a woman's prerogative. When we are late, we must deal with the drama but when they are late, we must function as if it is of no great concern.

 Gregory P. Williams

CHAPTER EIGHTEEN

Different Strokes For Different Folks

The thing about this guide is that you can tailor it to fit your particular needs. Some of us are naturally charming while others have to work a bit at it. Some of us know how to be chivalrous with others trying to be debonair.

My particular way is the poetic cowboy theme with a little charm and chivalry thrown in for good measure. We all have different ways of going about wooing said lady, as long as these rules are applied it really doesn't matter which way you go about it. I've seen guys swoop down on that pretty little thing while riding a skateboard while on the other hand, some guy's ride real hard in Benzo's and Maserati's... Just get out there and do it!

When you find your own style wear it like you would an old comfortable pair of jeans and don't be overly concerned about what others may say. As long as your clothes fit your attitude it's all good. The hip-hopster type does not look good in suits while the suave guy doesn't fill a pair of sagging pants all that well. Find out who and what you are and be that person. This guide is all about you finding you! So don't be trend followers, be trend-setters and make others want to be like you.

Don't be afraid to take out your highlighter and go over something that strikes your fancy. Some will get it in the first few chapters and others will find what they are looking for somewhere in the middle or the end. These are not hard and fast rules, only a guideline, a roadmap of what you should and shouldn't do.

As I mentioned earlier, the first part of the battle is to put a smile on her face and after that it's all gravy. On a warm day I might ask her if she wants to go get some ice cream or something. I may even go as far as to ask would she like to take a ride up to the lake for some beautiful scenery and a bottle of wine. It's whatever your imagination can conjure. Once she has fallen into your web of intrigue as it were, guide the conversation so that she is the one doing all the talking while you're paying attention to what she is saying so you can keep the conversation flowing smoothly.

Some women like the hot boy thing; your voice full of innuendo and surprise. Tantalizing her imagination with images of you and her together somewhere alone. You would be surprised at how many women like that approach. See, most guys like to take it too slow, and the girls have gotten used to that. First, they meet, then they talk for a while (a while being weeks or months) and then attempt to go in for the kill. I knew this one ShyGuy who had met this beautiful woman at the job we all worked at. She was all attracted to him, but he was moving way too slowly. I said to him "Dude, you have to move a little faster or that girl is going to get away". He angrily replied, "I take my time". And guess what? Yep, you got it, she got tired of waiting and the girl got away. So don't be afraid to make your move!

What I found with the majority of women I've been in contact with is that they appreciate an approach that's not bordering on stalled out. A faster than slow approach suits them just fine because you're not going at it like the other fellas, you're keeping it different. Just go for it and see where it leads.

The S.A.M. approach works in most cases most of the time I've found, but there will be those times when nothing seems to work. So

     Gregory P. Williams

don't get downhearted or anything because nothing is 100 percent effective. What we're doing here is getting up to around eighty percent, and eighty is outstanding! There will be periods when you can't miss, then there be times when you can't hit a lick but don't get discouraged because in the long run it will turn out alright for you. A friend's perspective is always something to have insofar as your personal growth is concerned.

They can sometimes see you better than you can. They will be the first to notice how you've changed and are continuing to change. Who are you now and who you are becoming is the question. If you're like most ShyGuys, when you first picked up this guide you were full of anxiety and apprehension about the opposite sex. Remember how terrified you were at the prospect of walking up to and talking to a stranger?

!f you've been doing your practice exercises, then your previous attitude toward girls should be past tense. You can now confidently articulate what exactly it is that you want from Ms Oh So Evasive. You can now bring her up to your level while communicating effectively and you'll notice too that your opinion of females in general is dramatically altered. No longer are they some hypothetical and conceptual being with unknown powers of the mind. They're just girls, and inconsistent in their thinking most of the time at that! You're arriving at that place called courageous and strong.

You've heard the phrase 'blowin' smoke' right? If you don't know what that means here we go; it means having the ability to come up with new and improved conversation on lightning tap, that is to say, at the drop of a dime. And let me tell ya fellas, the more smoke you blow at them the happier they seem to get, so get out your matches and light some fires. I was blowing smoke so hard at this one female that her eyes started to change colors and let me tell you, when I was done Ms Taken by Surprise was in a state of confusion in addition to being in my car!

As you become better and better at what you've been doing, tell a friend and bring another ShyGuy into the fold as it were. We ShyGuys need to stick together because there are people out there and I'm not dropping any names, Steve Harvey! Who is making it hard for us ShyGuys to get an even break out here. It was already difficult enough and then here he comes filling these girls' heads with a lot of unnecessary noise! That's okay because we've elevated the game to an entirely different level. So spread the word and let us become one united force!

Chapter Nineteen

Used Ta Bees Don't Make No Honey

My fellow ShyGuys, whatever you do don't end up being a 'used ta bee', because 'used ta bees don't make no honey'. And by that, I mean living on what you used to be doesn't bring anything to the table now. If you think that helps to win the girl, you're somewhat mistaken. Some girls are taken in by that but only some. Most of us are guilty of doing just that, including yours truly, but I've learned to pay careful attention to what I say.

I remember hearing this guy tell a girl all about that nice car he used to have and while he was telling her this, I noticed his chest swell up with pride. I also noticed that he was currently walking! I know a fella who used to be a pimp and on any given day he can articulate all the terms, philosophies and trickerations that go along with the game. It seems that at one time in his life he was surrounded by beautiful women waiting on his beck and call. Anything he wanted was at his fingertips.

He told me that he once had this woman here and that woman there, ranging from the San Francisco Bay to New York City and everywhere in between. While he was talking one day, I noticed that the cup he was drinking from was chipped, although it looked to have been expensive at one time, and you could see that his woman at one time was gorgeous but now she had small crow's feet around her eyes and was a bit chunky. And where once he had many women now, he had just the one. Yep, he's a used ta bee.

What does all this have to do with winning Ms Lovely? Everything. Because women don't particularly care for someone who used to be, they want someone in the now and not in the past. Besides, all of the money you used to have? Add a quarter to it and see if you can buy a cup of coffee.

While we're on the subject of used ta bees, let us now explore the world of the girl used ta bee! yanno those girls you see wearing clothes that are way too tight? Well fellas, those clothes used to fit! Here she is styling and profiling as if she is still that hot body girl she used to be.

Sometimes we have to put them in a holding pattern and give them a reality check, 'hey girly, you might have been all that a long time ago, but you need to climb down off that high horse cause you're not all that right now. You need to be happy I'm talking to ya! So take a chill pill and relax that noise.

I know of at least one girl who's happy to show you that pretty little outfit she used to wear but doggone it, it's hard to believe she ever got into that! Woman, you need to lay off the Cheetos, Zoozoo's and Wamwam's cause dayuum!

Having prestige once upon a time is way up on the list of what used ta bees like to talk about. "I used to be the senior manager at the bank" he said. Now fellas, although the charges of pilfering never stuck, he's now flipping burgers at the McDonald's down the way and still trying to ride high on his fifteen minutes of fame. The point being, be who you are right now and change for the better. It's absolutely hysterical to listen to a guy tell a girl about all the game he has, and for those who don't know, game is that well thought out and slick way of talking that you do without letting anyone be the wiser. But the thing is, he's talking like it was ten years ago instead of right

     Gregory P. Williams

now. Partner, that particular game went out with platform shoes, oh damn, you say platforms are back in play? Oops, my bad.

I have a real good friend and when he reads this, he'll probably say something like, "Imma bust you in the head and when you get out of the hospital, it'll be just about the time I'm getting out of jail and I'm gonna bust you in the head again cause I'm stupid like that!" And the reason for all that is that game is bought and not taught, sold, and not told (as he puts it) and he'll want his royalties for me putting him in this guide, and when I tell them there are no royalties, well... See, my buddy used to be a gangster and not a gangsta.

I don't mean the pants sagging till their behinds show variety. I'm talking about the bonafide, certified silk suit wearing for real type. At times he'll expound on his long-ago activities and sometimes I have to stop him and remind him of used ta bees, by the way, he's one who told me that phrase... Just to give him his mack.

Another friend of mine used to have a home designed for giving parties and that's just what he did, gave parties and played some old blues because he's one of my older friends and that's what he listened to as a young man. You can catch him now at home in his office listening to old blues and thinking about times gone by.

Okay it's my turn. My fellow ShyGuys, I can talk about other people because I used to be a real debonair dresser then one day, I realized that I was a used ta bee! I then went out and bought a whole new wardrobe because mine was somewhat dated! At one time I was as guilty as the next guy of being a used ta bee. I used to captivate my listeners (and that's what they were ... captive; they came to visit, and I locked the door!) With stories of my wild, misspent, and wayward youth. I reveled in the glory of fine dining and fancy cars, beautiful women in upscale bars, lighting $100 cigars with fifty-dollar bills. Yep, I had no sense whatsoever. Then one day I realized those days were long gone and all that was left of them was me.

The same goes for education. I've attended several colleges and like to think of myself as being well read and versed. But I have to remember that was thirty years ago and what I learned back then has little bearing on what's going on now. The electronics I learned? Well, I can still fix a computer better than most. But not down to the component level the way I used to. I can still write, but there are times when some of the terms I use are archaic to say the least. So please forgive me if an old word or two pops up here and there!

Gregory P. Williams

Chapter Twenty

A Scared Man Can't Gamble and a Jealous Man Can't Work

Have you heard the old adage about how a scared man can't gamble and a jealous man can't work? A scared man is afraid of losing hence he can't gamble. While a jealous man can't work for the exact same reason -fear. Fear of losing his lady love to the mail carrier or maybe the milkman or it could be that fella down at the grocery store.

And just like the scared man who is so fearful of losing that he will not make a bet on an almost sure thing, the jealous man is so afraid of someone looking at or talking to his woman that he can't hold a job. Because he always has the need to be near her so he can keep an eye on her, he can't leave home for long periods!

Be it the would-be gambler or the jealous guy, it all boils down to fear. Although in the case of the jealous guy he's also so insecure and lacking self-confidence, that he literally can't work! It makes him too nervous to be away from her. We ShyGuys have learned that if we are confident in ourselves and our ability to get and keep a woman, we can work and gamble until our hearts are content!

What is it in a man's psyche then that makes for fear of another man insofar as his own woman is concerned? Is it because he had made love to that woman and knows her every moan and groan, the way her body moves and feels and then the thought of another man doing the exact same to her? Or she doing those things to him?

On the other hand, maybe there is an innate lack of trust for women in general which goes back to fear. Maybe he's feeling guilty and thinks that she is doing what he's doing -that is if he's doing something undercover.

All the above is certainly true although it doesn't have to be. Trust in yourself and what you're doing. You know that your game is strong and that the only way she will go to another is because she is a sorry excuse of a woman. So don't take it to heart if something like that does happen, she will end up being the loser in that situation. Besides, that cutie at the clothing store has been making eyes at you! So, you want to know if you're the jealous type or not. Most people will not come out and say it, so you have to look for little telltale signs in your character makeup.

- Do you have the need to know where she is at all of the time? Every hour, every minute and every second?
- Are you irritated when she sleeps over with the girls?
- When other men look at or speak to her does that make you a tad bit uncomfortable?
- Do your romances tend to not last very long?

If you answered yes to either of these questions, odds are you are the jealous type. Yep, that green eyed monster is just waiting to be let off his chain. Side note: not to make too fine a point, but some of those characteristics puts you squarely in the sociopathic arena. Just as an added note, I once saw a man stabbing a box of cereal and he asked me "what am I?" And I replied, "I dunno, cereal killer?" Okay, bad serial killer pun. The point is, keep that green eyed monster in check. And as my sister is fond of saying, "ya need Jeezus!"

Conclusion & Summary

As we have discovered, getting the girl has never been easier. We have found that our looks really don't have a whole lot to do with it although we've also found that using all the bait at our command greatly increases our odds of success. Getting the girl seems to be getting simpler and simpler as we utilize the tools now in our toolbox.

By now we've gone through several women of the various types and personalities and have concluded that yes, they truly are street rat crazy! Like I said previously, they're about as predictable as rain is on a real cloudy and overcast day. If we want them to go left, we in our quiet way suggested they go right!

Perhaps you've executed your plan with such clarity and precision that you now have Ms Yes Indeed by your side, and if you only wanted one-night stands, by now you have had several of those. Whatever the case, have all the fun that you've earned and deserve.

We've gone over S.A.M. (Say Anything Method) in some detail and that is where those thirty seconds come into play. You have just about that much time to impress Ms Hey Girl to the point that she will want to continue talking to you.

When I say that you can say just about anything, that's exactly what I mean. Just make sure you keep it in the context of who you're talking to. Now, if I've approached a hood rat, I know that my language can be somewhat coarse. Alternately, if I'm dealing with the good girl type I know how to keep it somewhat and reasonably clean. By contrast, when talking to the gold digger, I know that she will accept a lot more from me because her eyes are shining from looking at my pot of gold!

The Say Anything Method is at the core of attracting that lovely vision. It's here that you come up with something different from what she is accustomed to hearing. Remember, each time you step to a woman those are the most critical thirty seconds of your life. Keep it original! "All the world's a stage and all the men and women merely players, they all have their exits and entrances, And one man in his time plays many parts.

The great bard Shakespeare wrote those prophetic lines and it's appropriate to us ShyGuys who are now social butterflies. When we come on stage, that is, whenever we walk out of the front door, we must have our best face on ready to play our part of the suave and smooth person we're becoming. Dressed to impress and impeccable in our attire, choosing our bait carefully. We smell sweeter than a gold digger out on the hunt and we're ready for whoever should step into our light.

Yanno, we don't know when, where or under what circumstances that special lady will come into our lives and so we must always maintain the look that we know and are certain to attract her attention. Opportunity is a sly caller who comes knocking at your door but sometimes the back door and often times a quiet knock so we must always be prepared.

I remember once while living in the San Francisco Bay Area, I pulled up to a hamburger joint and standing there was one of the loveliest women that I had ever seen. I had just left home and was wearing some cutoff jeans and T-shirt; my hair wasn't combed so I threw on a skull cap. I had my little sister with me and so I asked her to say to that woman "my brother isn't really dressed to be out in public and would she come over to the car. Surprisingly enough she came over and I said to her, "I don't normally accost strange women

     Gregory P. Williams

on the street but" and she replied, "so you think I'm strange?" I smiled "you have this strangely haunting inner beauty radiating from your eyes". (SAM) we started dating after that! But like I said before, you never know when or where. If you've been practicing being your charming best by now you should have an abundance of it!

You've been practicing walking up to women and making them smile and feel comfortable in your presence. Each time you have a success it gives your ego a boost and along with that your self-confidence. Don't worry about the times when you're not successful, just take it as a learning experience to be dissected to see what you could've done better.

Friends and family may even start commenting on your behavior, noticing that you smile more, stand a little taller and are an all-around different person. You yourself will notice a change in your basic personality. No longer are you afraid to step up to a woman and make your play. If she says yes then that's all well and good, but if she says no then say to yourself, get out of line miss next!

We talked about how getting the girl is a numbers game. If you concentrate on one or two girls, you may or may not get one. But if you talk to fifteen or twenty, you're bound to strike gold! It's a mathematical certainty that the more women you talk to the greater your odds of success.

We went over fishing different streams and how that also increases your success rate. The Internet is a great place to fish so to speak. Another good place is the cruise ship. Try different places and talk to as many as you can, just be sure not to act hungry, women can sense that. Just be friendly and they'll never know that you're laying traps to be checked later!

The biggest obstacle standing in your way is ... You. Don't believe me? Then take a step forward and then turn around and look at yourself! You know about the different types of girls and their personalities; you know what they want and what they think they can't have. You also know that if you pay too much attention to them, they'll run.

So, if you've done your homework there's absolutely nothing that can stop you except you. You can stand in your own way by being afraid of the girl. Remember she is just a girl, no big deal. You can put the brakes on yourself by not believing in yourself. You can act hungry, and you already know what that means ... desperate.

In other words, if you do everything the exact opposite of what you learn here you can easily sabotage yourself! Just remember that doing things the way you were going about it didn't work out too well so try something different. Doing the same thing repeatedly and expecting a different result is somewhere in the realm of crazy I've been told. Do differently; act differently, be different!

Before going out there we need to think out clearly which species we're going after. If I want a saltwater fish, it isn't likely I will find one in fresh water. Know who and what you're going after. There is a cornucopia out there fellas, of wants and desires just waiting for you to appear and claim your share!

For my fellow ShyGuys who're looking for that elusive wife just know that there is an excess of willing and compliant wives out there waiting for you to introduce yourself. And for my ShyGuys who prefer playing the field all I have to say is 'play on ShyGuy, play on! There are more one night stands out there than there are days in the year. So, if you prefer, you can enjoy one night stands a couple times a night! The only limitations are those you set for yourself!

Confidence is something that can be learned by anyone if they're willing to take a few risks, namely, the risk and fear of rejection. Rejection doesn't always mean no; it just means that she needs to know more about you and what you're talking about! The more she learns about you the sooner that initial no will turn into a yes.

At this stage of the game, it's getting harder and harder for women to causally discard your charismatic mannerisms and flair; you're direct and poised, a charmingly delightful person to be around. Like

     Gregory P. Williams

I always say, if she insists on no being her answer that's fine ... Next! Keep it movin' like a freight train because somewhere down the line the one that you were made for will show up and be drawn to your magnetic personality, captivated by your wit and almost magical style ... and you hers!

The question I seem to get asked mostly by ShyGuys is 'by using your method will I win her every time?' And my answer is a categorical NO! No one, not even the fabled and legendary Don Juan was batting one hundred percent so come on in and join club! As we talked about earlier it's simply a matter of numbers. The more numbers you accumulate the greater your successes will be.

People in business carry their business cards while those socializing carry what I like to call social cards bearing my name and contact information. I will add something tantalizing like 'the dream maker' on the back and get responses like "and what dreams do you make come true?" And the like. That's another time when I use S.A.M. I might answer with something like "what's your fantasy?" Yep, I go straight for the panties. You'd think that I'd have grown out of that by now but hey, I still have my amorous side!

Don't let looks be your indicator of whether or not this girl or that girl is the right one for you because there are pretty girls with downright ugly personalities and not so pretty girls with absolutely charming personalities.

For me the pretty scale somewhat comes into play, but the fun meter is where I make my final decision; is this girl fun to be around. An entertaining and seductive nature is what I mostly respond positively to. But hey like I said, I'm not trying to go out with the wolfwoman either. I know, that's so shallow ... I'm just trying to keep it real cause I can't keep it right. My personal indicator is whether or not I can walk with her by my side and still be able to hold my head up!

It's just like the Boy Scout motto: always be prepared. I cannot stress that enough. See, the very moment you're not ready is when Ms

Waiting all my Life will pop up and she will be looking good. Just the other day I jumped into my ride to run down to the corner store (I was not prepared to meet anyone) who do you think pulled up beside me? Yep, you got it. So I rolled down my window, gave her my most dazzling smile and put in thirty seconds worth of work. It worked. Alas, in my present situation I couldn't take advantage of it, so I left her for one of you to bedazzle!

Now this was a singular moment because most times it doesn't work that way for most people not ready for it. So stay prepped. I've been doing this for so long that I can rattle off some SAM at a moment's notice. With practice, you'll be able to also.

I'm sometimes asked, "what's the best bait out there?" and I answer with "the one thing you carry with you at all times ... you". You're the best bait out there, everything else is an accessory. That personality you've been working on? It's better than bling. A charming and glowing inner self will make you shine like a pot of gold. You'll put on a pair of jeans and people might think you're wearing a tux! The clothes don't make the man look good; the man makes the clothes look good.

Use all your bait. Don't slouch. Stand up straight and tall and people will think you're taller than you actually are. I get that all of the time. When you happen to meet her eyes from across the way or while passing by, give her that beaming smile you've been working on. And when she passes closely by she will get a hint of that cologne you're wearing and will probably think of you off and on throughout her day and if you were bold enough to have her take a pause in her day, you just might end up with those digits!

If you haven't done so already it's time to get out there and work on your program. I know from experience that going from ShyGuy to social butterfly can be a scary thing but don't worry. You've done everything right. You've practiced that brilliant smile and charm. All you need now is to have faith in yourself, faith that you are becoming the man you want to be, and you're just getting better.

     Gregory P. Williams

When I first stepped out, I went on a jazz cruise and talk about women being everywhere! I wanted to try a place I'd been told was pretty much easy work and they were right. Girls were making eyes at me from the time the ship took off and so I followed my program.

1. Don't act hungry.
2. Smile, wink and be charming.
3. Dress for the occasion.
4. Prowl the ship's night clubs.

I had more fun than I ever thought I would. Women were throwing themselves at me anytime I left my cabin. I've found over the years that any place women congregate for good times and fun is the place to be. So get on out there and be who you are.

Okay fellas, now that you're having the time of your life don't screw it up by falling for one of these manipulative, money chasing, stiletto wearing barracudas out there! There are way too many women to sample before settling down for just the one.

There are so many types of women to interact with, so many personalities to contend with. It's just like buying a car or a house; you would have to test drive a few before you find one that fits you. You wouldn't buy the first house you looked at either, you'd look at and consider many.

Having one woman or multiple women intimately in your life can be a lot of fun but it's also fascinating to watch ... It's wilder than a reality TV show. Be it her or them, your life will be filled with intrigue. Yes, my fellow ShyGuys, don't think that woman or those women aren't somewhere plotting some scheme to find out just how much loot you have and where it currently resides!

Oh yeah, they'll gently and tenderly stroke your heart with one hand while stealthily reaching for your wallet with the other. They know that they have a gold mine down there and they know just how to make it produce gold bullion!

This isn't the end my fellow ShyGuys, it's just the beginning of a new and delightful life filled with intrigue, astonishment, laughter, humor and when you find that perfect lady love ... magic. Someone once said that 'the journey of a thousand miles begins with but a single step' and here you are taking that first step toward an enjoyable and hopefully long-lasting voyage.

I've had a lot of fun writing this guide and hopefully you're having a lot of fun using it. Yanno, I endured a lot of good-natured razzing from all sexes. One person wanted to hang me in effigy from a tall building for my apparently reckless and insensitive observations!

I sincerely hope that the information contained here will be of some value to you on your road to happiness. I truly hope this guide not only imparts helpful tips in your love life but in life in general. With your new found courage, faith, and self-confidence you can conquer whatever it is you set your mind to. You may find that these fundamental principles have a useful place in many areas of your multi-faceted life. So good luck in your adventures and may the power and love of infinite intelligence always find a way into your hearts and minds.

Until next time.

Gregory P